Books by Ian Southwell

Born of the Spirit:
Helping Seekers Enter and Grow in God's Family (2009)

Prayer:
The Communication of Love (2010)

Giving to God:
A Response of Love (2011)

Holiness:
A Radiant Relationship (2012)

(Stairways Series, Published by Salvo
Publishing, Melbourne, Australia)
www.salvationarmy.org.au/supplies

Safely Led to Serve:
A Joint Biography (2017)

(With Sonja Southwell, Published by Balboa
Press, Bloomington, IN 47403, USA)

www.balboapress.com.au

Lasting Treasu

The Story of George and Jennie

Ian Southwell

Lasting Treasure

The Story of George and Jennie Lonnie

Ian Southwell

BALBOA.
PRESS
A DIVISION OF HAY HOUSE

Balboa Press books may be ordered through booksellers or by contacting:

Balboa Press
A Division of Hay House
1663 Liberty Drive
Bloomington, IN 47403
www.balboapress.com.au
1 (877) 407-4847

Print information available on the last page.

ISBN: 978-1-5043-1607-1 (sc)
ISBN: 978-1-5043-1608-8 (e)

Balboa Press rev. date: 12/17/2018

To my family
and to all who are desiring fresh inspiration
in their service for God.

G. W. LONNIE.

December 25th 1909.

The World crowns –
Success;
God crowns –
Faithfulness.

Flyleaf of George Lonnie's Bible, 25 December 1909

Lieut-Colonel George Lonnie and
Mrs Lieut-Colonel Jennie Lonnie, c. 1943

Contents

Contents

Some readers' comments

In these days of modern travel and technology it is inspiring to be reminded of 'pioneers' of other days who expressed their faith, determination, courage and fortitude in their following of God's call on their lives. To read of their passion to encourage all they met to accept Jesus Christ personally and then to go on in their discipleship to share that faith with others is challenging to us in our day.

For any of us appreciating the vast distances across Western Australia we cannot help but marvel at all that was achieved by George and others involved in this pioneering ministry in harsh and demanding conditions.

Reading on, when George was joined in his work and service by Jennie, as well as Jennie's prior ministry, one's admiration for them both and their ministry across Australia and New Zealand only increases. Eternity itself will reveal all that was accomplished by these faithful and courageous servants of God.

K. Brian Morgan, Commissioner
Australia
December 2018

Thank you for the opportunity to read this delightful and impacting story of George and Jennie Lonnie. What courage and dedication the whole story is immersed with. It is a history largely lost to modern Salvationists and so your recording of it is so important. It is difficult to appreciate in today's society just how tough life was for those early officers and their families. I think the script reads well and is an interesting and inspiring read.

Thanks for undertaking this work. It is a good addition to the Army history in New Zealand and Australia.

Campbell Roberts, Major
New Zealand
September 2018

George and Jennie Lonnie's singleness of mind and commitment to their calling and the mission of The Salvation Army is truly inspirational.

Given the challenge of resources and transport of the day, their determination saw many, many people led to the Lord as they travelled both in Australia and New Zealand. God blessed their ministry and provided for them as a family even through the loss of close family members while they were away from their home country.

They were truly pioneers in their own right but were able to accomplish the mission with the help of many others along the journey and in so doing left a remarkable heritage for their families and The Salvation Army.

Garry Mellsop, Major
New Zealand
September 2018

Preface

'... our hearts were greatly cheered when our first soul sought salvation. This dear fellow had travelled all the way from Melbourne in search of the gold that perishes. He failed to find this, but found instead the pearl of greatest price!'

So wrote George Lonnie of the earliest days of his work at Southern Cross, Western Australia, in 1893. He and his companion, Captain Charles Bensley, had walked 152 km east over four solid days from the end of the railway line to that mining settlement in hot, dry and dusty conditions. Having built their own accommodation and a meeting hall using saplings cut from the bush, hessian and discarded wooden crates, it took seven weeks of faithful teaching, preaching and caring for the needs of the prospectors there before that first soul sought and found the lasting treasure of salvation.

Born on the goldfields of Victoria, Australia, in the latter half of the 19th century, George Lonnie and Jennie Hammer made the same great discovery—lasting treasure—a relationship with God through Jesus Christ. First individually, and then as a couple, they shared their discovery by proclaiming the gospel and alleviating human needs through Christian ministry in The Salvation Army in Australia and New Zealand. In so doing they experienced precious strength to face privations, illnesses, bereavements and disappointments—as well as exciting times of great joy. The story of their resilience and courage is both challenging and inspiring.

Jennie Lonnie was my maternal grandmother and lived with my parents and me for 11 of the first 12 years in my life. She was a gracious and refined lady who spoke well, enjoyed reciting poetry, and telling or reading stories to her grandson. Above all, she loved her Lord and Saviour, Jesus Christ. She was a great encouragement to me in all of my studies and Salvation Army involvements as a young person over those years from 1943 until 1954, even as her eyesight failed and health declined.

On occasions, she would tell me of the exploits and hardships faced by my grandfather, George Lonnie, especially on the goldfields of Western Australia where he helped to pioneer Salvation Army activity in the 1890s. She mentioned only little of her own service as a single officer in social services to women and girls in Melbourne and Adelaide before her joint service with George around Australia and in New Zealand.

Like most grandchildren, I now regret that I did not ask her more questions or seek more details about their lives. Perhaps she assumed that my mother would tell me more—and to some extent, she did.

It is only since my own retirement from active Salvation Army officer service that I have commenced some in-depth research into the lives of George and Jennie Lonnie. As I have done so, I have been inspired by their determination, tenacity and total dedication to God and sharing the gospel despite many personal sorrows and other challenges. No doubt, their stories are not unique in regard to early-day officers (ministers) of The Salvation Army in Australia and New Zealand. But I believe this story is worth recording to inspire and encourage present-day Salvationists and Christians of other denominations in their dedication to God. Such details should not be left in archival files at a heritage centre or museum. Hopefully, all readers will learn, in the words that George Lonnie so often penned in autograph books and which were inscribed on the flyleaf of his Bible: 'The world crowns success; God crowns faithfulness.'

As George and Jennie Lonnie told and wrote of some of their experiences from time to time, and these accounts were published in Salvation Army periodicals, I have quoted their own words where I can so that you can discover something of their passion for God and the nature their ministries. Elsewhere, I have drawn from reports of their lives gleaned from the pages of *The War Cry* in Australia and from similar resources in New Zealand.

Because all their service for God was within the context of The Salvation Army, I have included a 'Glossary of Some Salvation Army Terms and Abbreviations' at the conclusion of the book from page 113 as well as occasional explanations in the main text. I hope these will serve to assist those not familiar with some terminology I may take for granted.

My prayer is that you will find inspiration, challenge to service and encouragement to continue serving God faithfully as result of reading this account.

Ian Southwell, Lieut-Colonel
Melbourne, Australia
January 2019

Acknowledgements

This book could not have been completed in a timely manner without research by George Ellis, sometime Territorial Archivist for The Salvation Army in the Australia Southern Territory and now retired. George meticulously analysed copies of *The War Cry* from the 1890s to 1943 whilst personally researching the history of Melbourne City Temple (now Melbourne Project 614). At the same time, he also diligently searched for and copied reports linked to the names Lonnie and Hammer, together with similar information about the Sharp and Southwell families. I owe George a great debt of gratitude.

I am also grateful to the present Territorial Archivist, Lindsay Cox, together with Major Donna Bryan and Dot Skewes of his staff, for individualised support for this book, including the access that they made possible for George Ellis to the many volumes of *The War Cry* in recent years. Dot Skewes' grandfather—Harry Jorgensen—was led to the Lord in Western Australia in the 1890s by George Lonnie and she has shown special interest in and support for this project. The team responded to my many detailed questions. Lindsay also granted me permission to reproduce articles, illustrations and photographs from Salvation Army publications of the period.

William (Bill) S. Booth, who from 2000 until 2010 was in charge of The Salvation Army Heritage Museum in Western Australia, was a great source of information about George Lonnie's and later the couple's service in that State. Together with Envoy Tom Fernihough, he was a pioneer of The Salvation Army Historical Society in Western Australia which I was pleased to inaugurate in 1993 whilst Divisional Commander.

The Heritage Centre and Archives for The Salvation Army in New Zealand, Fiji and Tonga Territory, currently led by Sharon Burton together with Selwyn Bracegirdle, Research and Content Manager, have given wonderful support in unravelling several important details of the Lonnies' service in New Zealand. The team there carefully extracted relevant information for me over several years from the New Zealand editions of *The War Cry*.

Divisional staff and corps historians from around Australia and New Zealand also responded to my requests for information dating back to when I commenced this research in 2008. Thank you for taking the time to do so.

I am also grateful to the staff of the Family History Research section at the Burke Museum in Beechworth, Victoria for information they were able to share with me about the Lonnie and McCarter families.

A number of knowledgeable readers have made comments about the manuscript, suggesting alterations and improvements in addition to giving their own recommendations. Amongst these are Commissioner K. Brian Morgan and Major Brad Halse from Australia, and Major Campbell Roberts and Major Garry Mellsop from New Zealand. Their help is much appreciated and also their permission to include their recommendations within the book and in summary on the back cover.

I am also deeply grateful to my wife, Sonja, and my daughters, Sharon and Jenni, for carefully reading through the script, and making suggestions about the contents and style. Having read the whole manuscript, Sharon recommended a change to my draft title of 'Faithful Followers'. Her husband, Greg Restall, produced the cover design.

I am most also grateful to my friend Dawn Volz, of The Salvation Army Literary Department and Ringwood Corps, for carefully reading and checking the manuscript and proofs.

The staff of Balboa Press have also greatly assisted in producing an attractive volume, especially Gemma Ramos (Check-In Coordinator), and designers, editors etc.

My thanks to you all.

Illustrations Acknowledgements

Cover photograph

Wedding photograph of George and Jennie, January 1901, taken by Mathewson & Co. Studio, then Brisbane, now 20 Rangeview Road, Toowoomba, Qld., 4350, Australia, and used with their permission.

Cover Design

© 2018 'Lasting Treasure' by Greg Restall, used with his permission, September 2018.

Author Photograph (page 121):

© 2006 Photograph courtesy Tony Isbitt, Bromley, Kent, UK, used with his permission, October 2018.

Other Illustrations and Photographs:

Scan of flyleaf of George Lonnie's Bible in possession of the author and scanned by him (page vii).

Lieut-Colonels George and Jennie Lonnie c. 1943, from the author's private collection and family photograph album (page ix).

Artist's representation of the hall in Southern Cross which accompanied *The War Cry* article, 7 April 1928, used with permission of The Salvation Army Heritage Centre - Melbourne (page 15).

Photo of George Lonnie's prospector scales and weights for measuring gold dust given as 'collections', © 2018 Ian Southwell (page 19).

Artist's representation of the hall at Coolgardie from *The War Cry*, 10 February 1894, used with permission of The Salvation Army Heritage Centre - Melbourne (page 20).

Photograph of first school in Coolgardie set up by Lieutenant George Lonnie, provided from The Salvation Army Western Australia Archives and used with their permission (page 21).

The War Cry artist's 1931 representation of Captain George Lonnie and Lieutenant John Powell trying to arrange alternative and safe accommodation for the motherless girl, which accompanied a story by George Lonnie in the 7 November 7 1931 edition, used with permission of The Salvation Army Heritage Centre - Melbourne (page 26).

Captain George Lonnie and his bicycle, c. 1897, from the author's personal collection (page 33).

Adelaide War Cry boomers (sellers) *The War Cry*, 6 May 1899, used with permission of The Salvation Army Heritage Centre - Melbourne (page 34).

Young People's Sergeant-Major Jennie Hammer, 1896, from *The War Cry* 1896, used with permission of The Salvation Army Heritage Centre - Melbourne, having been repaired by Camera House, 125 Main Street, Croydon, Vic. Australia (page 38).

Adelaide Slum Sisters, 1899 (Jennie Hammer is second from the left), from *The War Cry* 1899, used with permission of The Salvation Army Heritage Centre - Melbourne (page 40).

Wedding photograph of George and Jennie, January 1901, taken by Mathewson & Co. Studio, then Brisbane, now 20 Rangeview Road,

Toowoomba, Qld., 4350, Australia, and used with their permission (page 42).

Adjutant and Mrs Lonnie with Captain Mary Anderson (centre), from *The War Cry*, 24 February 1906, used with permission of The Salvation Army Heritage Centre - Melbourne (page 45).

Christchurch Corps Lasses Band c. 1905 with Adjutant George Lonnie and Bandmaster Tom Young, from *The War Cry,* 30 December 1905, used with permission of The Salvation Army Heritage Centre - Melbourne (page 50).

Florence (left) and Ivy Lonnie (right) c. 1909, from the author's personal collection (page 57).

Candidates from Sydney 1 Corps in 1911, with Staff-Captain George Lonnie, from *The War Cry,* 14 October 1911, p. 3, used with permission of The Salvation Army Heritage Centre - Melbourne (page 61).

The Lonnie family, 1927, from left: Florence, George, Ivy and Jennie, taken by Croxton Studio, High Street, Thornbury, Victoria, in 1927, company now out of business (page 78).

'Will you decide for officership today?' from *The War Cry,* 27 August 1927, p. 8, used with permission of The Salvation Army Heritage Centre - Melbourne (page 84).

Wedding reception for David and Florence Southwell at the Lonnie's Thornbury, Victoria, home, 29 December 1934, with Mrs Field-Major Sarah Southwell at left and Mrs Lieut-Colonel Jennie Lonnie at right, from the author's personal collection and possibly taken by his uncle, Allen Sharp (page 95).

Jennie Lonnie and the author as a boy, on possibly her 83rd birthday in 1953 from the author's personal collection and possibly taken by his mother, Florence (page 99).

CHAPTER 1

The carpenter from Yackandandah

Perhaps the potato famine in the 1850s in the British Isles was one factor in encouraging people to look for better living conditions elsewhere—especially in the British colonies. Certainly, the discovery of gold at Clunes, north of Ballarat in 1850, and subsequently in other parts of Victoria, also brought an influx of immigrants to the State. Amongst them were the Lonie family (later known as Lonnie) from Fifeshire in Scotland and the McCarter (or McCarty) family from Cumberland in north-west England.

Gold was discovered near Spring Creek in Beechworth in 1852 and, before long, alluvial deposits were found along Yackandandah Creek—a small tributary of the north-flowing Kiewa River. Small settlements sprang up and mining communities developed along its banks including Osbornes Flat, Allans Flat and the township of Yackandandah itself.

The 21-year-old William Lonnie staked a gold-mining claim in Beechworth in 1856, then moved to the Yackandandah area 32 km to the north-east in 1857. In August 1858, William married 18-year-old Isabel McCarter at Osbornes Flat. While William toiled to find gold—at times individually but also as a labourer for a Mr T. Riley—Isabel raised a large family. Twelve children were born to William and Isabel between June 1859 and January 1883 at either Osbornes Flat or Allans Flat. George William Lonnie (henceforth named George Lonnie) was their fifth child, born on 10 November 1866.[1]

In 1856, the Church of England established a school for the growing number of children at Osbornes Flat. By 1858, the official enrolment was 27, with 16 boys and 11 girls making up this total. The school existed for 18 years and was eventually closed in October 1874. George Lonnie probably commenced his schooling there. In 1872 an application was made to the Board of Education in Victoria for a Common School. Significantly, George's father, William Lonnie, was a member of the local committee brought together to plead for the new school. With two or three surviving school-aged children in his family at that time, including eight-year-old George, William and Isabel were keen that their children and others in the district had the opportunities for education. (At least two older siblings of George died before they were five years of age.) In November 1873, tenders were received for a new State School and this was built on a four-acre area prior to its official opening in 1874.[2]

It was at Yackandandah where George first met The Salvation Army. Having commenced in the East End of London in 1865 as an offshoot of the East London Special Services Mission, The Salvation Army had transitioned to the East London Christian Mission and then the Christian Mission. By 1878 the name of the organisation had changed to The Salvation Army. Soldiers (full members) of this 'Army' moved around the world, including to the relatively newly established colonies of South Australia, Victoria and New South Wales. The commencement of The Salvation Army in Australia is dated from Adelaide in September 1880. Trained officers were sent from England by William Booth, the Army's Founder, in 1881 to consolidate the ministry.

With Beechworth being a significant town in the then Ovens District of Victoria, which contained several significant goldfields in the State, it was logical that The Salvation Army commenced there in April 1884. When Captain (later Colonel) John Dean pioneered the work at Beechworth, he also ran an outpost at Yackandandah. He was followed in October 1885 till June 1886 by Captain E.B. Phillips.[3]

According to a story about George Lonnie in the Melbourne *War Cry*, 15 October 1910:

… amongst others who attended the meetings were members of the Lonnie family, including the lad George. Mrs Lonnie and a sister [of George] got converted, but though the captain tried to get George, he [Captain Dean] only succeeded in 'frightening six months' growth' out of him. During the next officers' term, that of the Happy Welshman (Staff-Captain Phillips), one of the greatest drunkards in Yackandandah got saved at the outpost. He was so full of new-found joy that he thought he would go to Beechworth (20 miles [32 km] distant) for the corps meetings on the Sunday, and invited George Lonnie to drive in with him. They went together, and at the night meeting Lonnie made his way, with a number of others, to the mercy-seat. Frequently, after this, the friends drove into meetings, returning in the small hours of the morning; and soon, getting a full grasp of salvation, Lonnie became a soldier.[4]

Sister Mrs Charlotte Kemp (nee Lonnie) was the sister of George who made her decision in 1883, some 58 years before her promotion to Glory in 1941. According to the report in *The War Cry*, her witness was so effective that 'seven members of the family became converted, Lieut-Colonel G.W. Lonnie (R) being among the number.'[5]

Following his conversion in 1886 (according to a New Zealand *War Cry* article in 1906 about the Christchurch Corps), George became thoroughly involved in Salvation Army service in his local corps, including helping the unsaved come to faith in Christ. As he wrote, 20 years later, 'As a young man I was a whole-hearted Salvation Army local officer, happy in God's work, able to lead others to the Cross.'[6]

He may well have been inspired by the enthusiastic evangelical outreach of The Salvation Army in those days. In 1888, a 'cavalry fort' called the *Conqueror*, consisting of horses and caravan, rolled out of Beechworth. Such cavalry forts transported enthusiastic Salvationists who took the gospel to remote areas. Despite a Salvation Army outpost having been established at Yackandandah some years before, author Barbara Bolton records that the *Conqueror* was assailed by a storm of rotten eggs in that township.[7]

Perhaps his parents' enthusiasm for education also encouraged George to move to Beechworth for some post-primary education and trade training. Carpentry and building skills would always be useful on the goldfields and elsewhere. George trained as a carpenter so that he could work as a contractor and earn some money for the family.

A crisis came for George, however. He continued his story:

> Then God called me to offer myself for training for officership. My parents were against this course, and my mother pointed out to me that my first duty was to honour and obey them.
>
> To this day I remember going [a]round to the officers' quarters, and there, in the front room, the two officers and I knelt upon the floor. But my choice was already made, and I said, 'No! I will obey father and mother, though it means disobeying God.' That moment something changed in my heart; I had lost my sanctification. It was as distinct and clean as the snapping of a thread.[8]

Not long after that, probably about 1887 or 1888, George left home and headed to Melbourne where he hoped to gain employment. An economic downturn and reduction in the profits of goldmining led to difficult times in rural and goldmining areas of Victoria. George moved to Melbourne and joined the Brunswick Corps.[9] George's enthusiastic Salvationist sister, Charlotte, had also moved to Brunswick and had married Joseph Kemp. So, George may have been able to live with them and their growing family.

George continued his account:

> For five years from that day [when he resisted God's call] my life was unhappy. I wore my uniform. The officers thought I was a good soldier but my heart knew no peace, my life no power. Not another soul did I win for God. Not

a holiness meeting did I enter without feeling condemned for my disobedience.[10]

Then one Friday night, as the comrades were singing—

I will not stop at the hearing,
what to my heart Thou shalt say,

my resistance broke down. The sacrifice I was then called upon to make was much greater than would have been the case five years earlier, but I surrendered fully. Three months later I led a young man to the mercy-seat—the first soul I had won in five years. As we walked up the aisle tears streamed from my eyes, and at that moment the glory of God came into my soul. I knew I was completely restored and from that date to this I have never been able to doubt the will of God for me.[11]

George then took the logical step of applying to become a Salvation Army officer. However, he required a doctor's certificate. One medical man, sensing a weakness in George's throat, said that two years of Army work would see him in his grave. Another doctor was more hopeful and, following some good advice, the trouble was successfully beaten. Seventeen years later (1910) George's counsel to other officers was: 'Abstain from sweets and gargle throat with vinegar and salt, and do not be afraid of cold water.'[12] This prescription certainly helped him to keep his voice in good condition to communicate the gospel as an officer for many years.

His Officer Career Card, written many years later,[13] indicated that he entered the Training Home, then situated in the Punt Road, Richmond, as a 26-year-old on 31.7.1893. However, his own record and a 1908 *War Cry* article indicates the date was 31.1.1893[14]—an easily explicable confusion between two similar numerals. While he was at the Training Home, George became an enterprising seller of *The War Cry*. 'He averaged 50 copies per week by his own personal effort.'[15]

As the 1908 article continues, 'After six happy months he received his promotion to the rank of Lieutenant, and was sent, with the late Adjutant Bensley, to open up the Yilgarn goldfields, WA.'

So by August 1893, the carpenter from the goldfields of Victoria was a commissioned Salvation Army officer and on his way to other goldfields on the opposite side of the continent.

CHAPTER 2

Pioneering in the West

In the Easter edition of *The War Cry*, 7 April 1928, and under the title of 'The Prospectors', George Lonnie told the story of his pioneering work for The Salvation Army on the goldfields of Western Australia. I reproduce it here with some minor editorial adjustments to keep the style consistent with the rest of this book. Also, in the text or through footnotes, I have given some explanations to help 21st-century readers understand the terminology that George Lonnie used.

> It was in the New Year of 1893 that I entered the old Training Garrison in Melbourne, and after only six months' training was selected as a pioneer for the Goldfields. With my yellow braid [the insignia of a lieutenant in those days] I received also the blessing of my leaders and my appointment to assist Captain Charles Bensley in the opening of Southern Cross, Western Australia.

> I commenced my long journey of over 3,000 miles [4,800 km] from Melbourne by boat. After nine days of considerable discomfort that can never be forgotten I reached Fremantle, scarcely able to stand. With my remaining energy I gathered my few things together and proceeded to the city of Perth, to hunt up the Divisional War Office. There I found Colonel Knight, who was then Staff-Captain, and in charge of Western Australia.

Having introduced me to my Captain, he gave instructions that we were to obtain a good supply of cheap underclothes, because we would be unable to get any washing done. This seemed rather strange to two young fellows from the State of Victoria who were accustomed to an abundance of water! We were told to proceed to Northam, a small country town 66 miles [106 km] from the centre, and there conduct the week-end meetings. A full day was put in, and a number of souls sought salvation. At this time Northam was the terminus of the Government railway line, and our destination lay 171 miles [274 km] further on, with no means of conveyance.

Next morning the Captain was astir seeking ways and means of getting away to the head of the line then under construction, from Northam to Southern Cross. At 8 am he came rushing back to my billet in a state of great excitement to acquaint me with the fact that the contractors' train would be leaving at 9.30 am, and if we were ready by that time we could obtain a lift at our own risk.

At that moment I was comfortably seated at the breakfast table and half-way through what would probably be the last decent meal I should enjoy for some time. However, begging of my hostess to be excused, I gathered together my few things, made them into a proper Australian "swag," and with a huge chunk of bread and butter in one hand made my way to the starting point. Our swags were made up of 6 x 8 tent [6 feet by 8 feet; or 1.8 m by 2.4 m], a rug each, a number of cheap shirts (purchased at 1/6 [15 cents] each), a few pair of socks, and other necessary articles, a tin billy-can, a couple of tin pannikins [metal drinking cups], a gallon [4.5 l] water-bag and a four days' supply of bread and meat. The rest of our belongings were packed into a case and handed over to a teamster with the promise that we should get them in a few weeks' time. Some of these promises stretched into months; but in due time they arrived, much heavier than when they were handed over having gathered dust galore.

In good time my Captain and I were both seated in a truckload of chaff that was bound for the head of the line (Doodlakine), the end of the construction, but 95 miles [152 km] from our destination. We reached Doodlakine at 5 pm and it had taken us seven and a half hours to cover 76 miles [122 km]. It was a very exciting trip. Several times our truck caught fire, also our clothes from the sparks that flew from the engine, which was stoked with wood. Still we did not mind; we had covered a good distance for the first day.

Arriving at the head of the line, we soon scrambled from our elevated position. What a wilderness we beheld! Navvies [low-paid labourers], horses, drays, wagons, camels, a few Aboriginals, numbers of dogs and abundance of steel rails and sleepers. There were a few shanties, a pub, a boarding-house and scores of tents.

This we all reckoned in our consecration and we were quite prepared to endure any hardness for Christ's sake.

Here we had our first experience of pitching a tent, boiling our billy and preparing our camp meal. Having no candles, we early decided to retire for the night. Removing our boots and rolling ourselves on our rugs we lay down on mother earth for our mattress. By the morning we felt stiff and more tired than when we retired the previous evening.

After a hurried breakfast an early start was made, this being necessary owing to the long distance between the watering places. The first few hours passed off very nicely, but by 12 o'clock we two city lads were feeling a wee bit tired and referred to the old tram cars we had left behind. Again, the billy was boiled. At 1.15 pm we were ready once more for the long, dusty road. With camels and horse trains constantly on the road there was an abundance of dust accompanied by swarms of flies. A little after dusk we reached the next watering place almost too tired to boil our billy and partake of our evening meal.

It was certainly interesting, and yet pitiful, to see the scores of poor horses, after their long, heavy journey in a glaring hot sun, clamouring for water. This precious commodity was served out very carefully, first in our billy-cans in readiness for tea, then in our water bags for the journey the next day.

Afterwards came the dumb animals. More than once a jam tin had to be used to fill the bucket to try and supply the needs of the horses.

After our evening meal we selected a clean spot to rest for the night. Thanking our Heavenly Father for the blessing of the day, and committing ourselves into his keeping, we lay down just as we were under the canopy of heaven for the night. Soon we were asleep, but not for long; our bones were not accustomed to such a solid mattress. Nor were we accustomed to the ants that seemed to take a special delight in running over us.

At daylight we were astir, getting ready for our second day's journey. Needless to say, we were not feeling as fresh as the previous morning. Clouds of dust and swarms of flies by day, ants at night and blistered feet as result of tramping rough roads, all helped to test our consecration and our love for the people whom we were seeking to save. One dry sandy lake 22 miles [35 km] across was most trying. Very thankful were we to our Heavenly Father when we reached the other side. What with the heat, flies and salt atmosphere, we were pretty well done.

Still, there were hundreds of other men who were risking all for the gold that perishes, therefore we would most gladly endure any inconvenience for the sake of those we are endeavouring to win for Christ.

Again, and again our hearts were stirred as we gazed upon the tribes of native blacks [Aboriginals] as they hung around the various camps longing for a drop of water to drink. The fact that the white man was commandeering the water soaks [water holes] to which they had previously had free access made it pretty bad for them, and their one plea would be 'Give us water!...'

Needless to say, the sight of two Army officers in uniform was a great mystery to these poor creatures. They certainly watched us from a distance, and thought we were some kind of policemen. When we conducted our open-air meetings, they thought we were holding a white fellows' corroboree, and it was not long before the black fellow passed around the hat for a collection.

At the end of four solid days' walking (and no eight-hour days either) we reached Southern Cross, our destination. We had hoped that it might be possible to find some friendly person who would take us in for a few days until we found our bearings, but what a dreadful surprise it was when at sundown on the Friday evening we reached the top of a small rise overlooking the town to discover a canvas town!

Four hotels, a post office, a bank, a police station and three or four stores were built of wattle and daub, one or two of iron and the rest of hessian [a coarse-weave cloth of fibre made from the jute plant]. The rest of the inhabitants lived in tents. The white population numbered four hundred, with very few women or children included. Weary and tired we made our way to the outskirts of the town, secured some poles from the bush around, selected a good level spot and set to work to erect our quarters.

One friendly storekeeper, hearing the Army had arrived, hunted us up, extended us a warm welcome and enquired if there was anything he could do for us. Were there any provisions that we required? For this we felt very grateful to God and thanked Him for our first friend.

Next day we moved around among the people and were made to feel by one and all that they were very glad to see us. We had to replenish our larder. There was not a great supply to choose from, everything being in tins—tinned meat, tinned vegetables, tinned fruit, and tinned puddings. The price almost took our breath away. Water was the most expensive commodity, being 1/6 [15 cents] per gallon, and very scarce at that. How we would have appreciated a few bucket fulls from the Yarra, if only for the sake of having a bath after a long, dusty journey of 95 miles [152 km]. We discovered that a shave would cost us 1/6 [15 cents], and a haircut 2/6 [25 cents] so we each decided to grow a beard!

Next night, at 7 o'clock, in the main street, we 'opened fire,' two strong with an old song 'We're travelling home to Heaven above—will you go?' By 8 o'clock we had fully 350 out of the small population for our congregation. How the crowds sang the old songs! Around the ring stood some of the brightest and best specimens of manhood from the leading mining centres of Australia. They knew the Army and its songs and loved its people and now felt they had a friend close at hand. The next day being Sunday, and having no hall, we held three open-air meetings. The attendance at night was simply wonderful, almost every living soul appearing to have turned out. They sang and sang, and listened to the old story of the Cross.

The offering was an eye-opener. Copper was very scarce. We had an agreement with the bank to let them have all the copper that came into our hands and they allowed us 3/- [30 cents] and sometimes 4/- [40 cents] on the £1

[$2]. The reason for the scarcity was the copper was too weighty and the escort too expensive to bring much that great distance.

On the Monday we had to arrange for furniture for our quarters. Not a stick could be bought for the place so it was a case of getting a few of the latest designs and making our own. It was impossible for us to lie on the ground night after night and to eat our food from the earth. The first and most important thing was a bed to lie on so with four forked saplings driven into the ground and two six foot [1.8 m] poles run through a couple of flour sacks, we completed our bunks, or rather our mattresses. Our overcoats and boots served as pillows, and our one rug was all the covering we possessed. And this is how we slept for a term of 15 months! Being six feet [1.8 m] tall, I found it a difficult matter to keep both ends covered at the same time owing to the rug measuring only five feet [1.5 m]. Our table, food safe, and easy chairs were made out of brandy and whiskey cases, or some other kind, with the words "Keep cool!" painted on them. Keeping cool, however, we found difficult.

Seeing there were no halls in the place, our next move was to obtain a block of land and arrange for a building of some sort in which to hold our meetings. Having secured a suitable block under a miner's right, there was still the question of building material. The only way open for us was to go into the bush and cut the necessary timber. Four days a week found the Captain and myself, with axes on our shoulders, a water-bag and a bit of lunch, wending our way three or four miles [five or six kilometres] into the bush to cut and dress timber for our citadel. This was a very trying ordeal, for my skipper, prior to becoming an officer, had been a compositor [printing typesetter]. However, we stuck to it, returned home each evening at sunset, boiled our billy, had a bit of tea, and then held an open-air meeting.

Having secured all the timber necessary, our next difficulty was to get it carted. It was impossible to hire a team. At last a friendly mine manager, who had been watching us closely, and admiring our pluck offered us a horse and dray if we could manage to drive, also to supply us with horse feed, a very big item in those times. Two trips a day soon got our material on to the spot where we were going to build our hall.

To get the post holes dug was the next problem. We certainly struck something much harder than we bargained for. With hands cracked, blistered and bleeding we toiled under a broiling hot sun, proved our stickability and finished the main building, a hall capable of seating two hundred people. It was built of saplings 13 feet 6 inches [4.1 m] long, 6 inches [15 cm] in the ground, nailed to the wall-plate at the top, lined inside with hessian and hessian again on the roof, as iron could not be procured. This was hot during the day, but cool for the evening.

To provide a platform and get seats was a next move, for not being able to get any timber suitable for our purpose we had simply to use our wits. For the platform we decided to erect the framework with saplings very close together and covered with boards from all kinds of cases that the storekeepers kindly gave us.

The platform complete, our minds turned to seating accommodation. What could we do to overcome the difficulty? We decided to get a sufficient number of small saplings, bore an auger hole through them, drive legs into them and make a kind of stool. Having made the required number of frames we were faced with the question of getting sufficient boards to cover them. These finished, we were again confronted with another difficulty. The ground not being level, the seats would not stand level. We decided to trust the weight of the occupants to bend them into shape! The crowd did not mind how lop-sided they were.

*Artist's representation of the hall in Southern Cross
which accompanied* The War Cry *article, 7 April 1928.*

Soul-saving was not an easy proposition; still, after seven
weeks' faithful dealing, and having just returned from a
hard day's work, our hearts were greatly cheered when our
first soul sought salvation. This dear fellow had travelled
all the way from Melbourne in search of the gold that
perishes. He failed to find this, but found instead the pearl
of greatest price!

Our first service of song and coffee supper—in fact, the first
ever held on the fields—turned out a great success in spite of
the tickets being 2/6 [25 cents] each. The hall was packed and
many were unable to gain admission. Special donations from
the supper were three kerosene tins of water, these being the
gifts of several young miners who denied themselves of so
much water each day out of their small allowance.

After an eight months' term, marching orders came and
we pushed our way on to Coolgardie, a distance of 130
miles [209 km] by road. This we covered by coach in three

days, each night being spent out in the open. By this time Coolgardie was a fine large town with a big population, but no religious organisation had yet commenced operations. The Army was the first.

Here we had a large hall erected on the same lines as Southern Cross; only that the seating was much more substantial; instead of having boarded stools we had logs, everything from six to 12 inches [15 to 30 cm] through, split up the centre, auger holes bored at each end and legs driven in and sawn off fairly level. These were very substantial, but not always satisfactory.

In some instances, we had the round side [of the log] up, in others the split side up. In the case of the round side there were occasional accidents, usually at the wrong time of the meeting. Each seat held eight adults, and perhaps one of the number, having taken a little too much drink, would over-balance. Throwing out his arms to save himself he would upset the whole row and instead of eight heads there would be sixteen feet visible. Needless to say, the uproar would be deafening.

When the split side was uppermost the seats were more comfortable, but now and then some restless individual would turn and twist around on his seat in such a way that when it came time to stand he found himself hooked to the seat by a splinter that it found its way through his Sunday trousers. Still, this did not prevent our hall being packed for almost every meeting.

To prevent overcrowding on the Sunday evening we would lock up our hall securely while we went to the open-air meeting, but would find on our return that the doors had been forced, the hall lighted up and packed to excess with miners singing for all they were worth. Many splendid conversions and soldiers [full members] were made. At times we would stand over 40 strong in the open-air with a nicely balanced band.

A few days later a new find [of gold] would be reported. Stores would be rushed for provisions and away would go the men, and we would be four or five strong. Often these reports of finds would turn out to be false, and in a few weeks the dear fellows would be returning bitterly disappointed. Some would never return, having laid down their lives in search for the precious metal.

The Army being the first on the Coolgardie fields we got a very good footing. There being no day school I decided to take the children from nine to twelve each day for school. There were only 27 all told; still, the parents were very grateful, and we secured them for our Juniors [Sunday school] every Sunday.

Seeing there were very few women on the fields, visiting was difficult but we moved about among the men who were dry-blowing[a] and endeavoured to lead them to the Saviour. Again, water was very scarce and we could never buy at less than one shilling [10 cents] per gallon [4.5 l], the result being we could only allow ourselves half pint [280 ml] each for our meals and one pint [560 ml] between us each day to wash in. The Captain would have the first wash morning in the clean water; after that, first come, first wash!

The first 15 months on the fields we were able to have only two thorough baths. On these occasions we had two heavy thunderstorms and were able to catch some extra water. Washing clothes was out of the question. On one occasion we secured enough second-hand water to wash

[a] Dry blowing is a method of extracting gold particles from dry soil without using water. It is a form of winnowing in which the denser gold particles tend to fall to the bottom of a container while the less dense soil particles are blown away by the wind. Because water was in such short supply on the Western Australian goldfields, dry blowing was the best option for extracting alluvial gold.

twenty-nine and a half pairs of socks. We usually went in for dry-blowing our clothes! Sickness and fever were very prevalent, and a good deal of our time was spent in caring for the poor chaps who were so far from home, and burying the dead. We also took our turn in assisting at the hospital at nights.

After a heavy rain storm, it was quite interesting to see hundreds of men out specking little bits of gold that had been washed up with the rain. On one occasion[16] the Captain and myself joined the party and collected sufficient gold with which we hoped to make wedding rings for the young women we hoped would make our wives. These rings they are wearing today.

Fresh food was almost out of the question and what with condensed milk and not too much of that, boils were no respecter of persons, so the police, parsons and public shared alike. First consignment of fresh eggs that arrived on the fields caused a sensation. There was a quick sale at 7/6 [75 cents] per dozen. The Army officers got a dozen for 4/6 [45 cents]. These were not very fresh but they were in the nature of the change and left no ill after-effects.

It has been my privilege since to return and travel over the same country, but oh! what a difference 30 years have made! Railway lines, motorcars, ample supplies of water, and beautiful wheat fields, where once was dreary desert country—the outcome of the blessings of our Heavenly Father upon the handiwork of man.[17]

In reading this fascinating account I was impressed with how well-equipped George Lonnie was for this task of pioneering Salvation Army work on the goldfields of Western Australia. His leaders made a good selection for this appointment.

He had demonstrated his enthusiasm to win souls for Lord both as a soldier and a local officer at Beechworth and Brunswick, and during his time in the Training Home. He identified with Paul that he saw the hardship they needed to face as 'hardness for Christ's sake'. Although arriving at Southern Cross on Friday night to discover most of the population living in tents, he and Captain Bensley found a spot to erect a quarters, obtained provisions and the very next day 'moved around among the people'. They understood that the basis of evangelism was personal contact and friendship. That Saturday night Bensley and Lonnie held an open-air meeting and 'officially' commenced Salvation Army work. The next day being Sunday, they held three open-air meetings because they did not yet have a hall to which to invite people.

While both of the officers brought a Bible, Charles Bensley brought his cornet to accompany the singing of songs that many of the prospectors obviously knew from the contacts with the church and The Salvation Army in the past.[18] From George's comments and contemporary photographs, in addition to Charles Bensley some prospectors had brought brass instruments to make music and entertain others. They could actually bring together a 'nicely balanced' brass band at times in Coolgardie. John Wesley, William Booth and our Lord would have been delighted. Bensley and Lonnie also believed all the world was their parish![19]

George Lonnie's prospector scales and weights
for measuring gold dust given as 'collections'.

While George described Captain Charles Bensley and himself as 'city lads', he omitted to mention what is outlined in Chapter 1: that he was born on the goldfields of Victoria. He would have seen the ways in which prospectors set up their accommodation. His knowledge of woodworking tools which he brought with him, his training as a carpenter and his experience as a contractor gave him both the knowledge and skills to be able to design beds to ensure a good night's sleep, build a quarters, and also a hall with enough seats to accommodate a crowd. With his converted friend from Yackandandah, George had learned to harness a horse and drive a dray with which to carry the materials back to the site of their hall.

Three months after Bensley and Lonnie commenced the work at Southern Cross, in September 1893, two other officers, Captain Edward Holman, and Lieutenant Ben Gardner were appointed to pioneer Army work in Coolgardie. Like their forerunners, they left the contractors train and walked to Southern Cross. Stopping for a day's rest, they saw the type of hall that Lonnie and Bensley had built. Travelling on a loaded wagon to Coolgardie, they built a similar hall there with cut timber and hessian. A sketch of The Salvation Army barracks in Coolgardie appeared in *The War Cry* of 10 February 1894.

Artist's representation of the hall at
Coolgardie from The War Cry, 1894.

Having been the beneficiary of a school set up by the Anglican Church at Osbornes Flat near Yackandandah, and the government school of which his father was an advisory board member, as mentioned in Chapter 1, George appreciated the value of education for children on the goldfields. In going to Coolgardie in 1894, he grasped the opportunity of commencing a school for the children of miners—even if it was initially just for three hours each day. Captain Bensley, who had been trained as a printer, would also have appreciated the benefits of a good education.

*Photograph of first school in Coolgardie
set up by Lieutenant George Lonnie.*

The photograph above of the first school students in Coolgardie came from the archives of The Salvation Army in Western Australia and was taken outside of the corps hall in Coolgardie. Lieutenant George Lonnie is at the rear left and Captain Charles Bensley at the rear centre. While there are 20 children in this group, in the later years of the 1890s the population grew so rapidly that a large stone State school was erected. Apparently by 1898, of the 500 children at the Coolgardie State School, not one was born in Western Australia. Eight out of every 10 came with their parents from Victoria.[20]

According to the results of research undertaken by Major Brad Halse, 'In February 1894 Bensley and Holman swapped places and then a few months later Lonnie joined his former captain at Coolgardie.'[21] So when the old team of Bensley and Lonnie got together again in May 1894, at least they had a hall from which to consolidate the work.[22] That was why George Lonnie was able to write in connection with Coolgardie, 'Here we had a large hall erected on the same lines as Southern Cross; only that the seating was much more substantial ...'. Nevertheless, George Lonnie's skills were pressed into service completing an extension to the Coolgardie barracks.

At least a substantially complete hall gave Bensley and Lonnie time to be involved in evangelism and caring for the many sick prospectors and their families in times when typhoid fever was rife.

Malcolm Uren records that, 'Captain [sic] Lonnie, besides being a nurse, had also to become undertaker. When the fever victims died he would look around for some old boxes, make a coffin, lay out the dead man, and then perform the burial service.'[23]

Uren goes on to share a touching memory of George Lonnie's ministry by a Mr Charles M. Harris, a long-term gold miner, nicknamed 'Diorite', as follows:

> One of the most poignant of Diorite's memories of the ministry of George Lonnie concerned the accumulated sadness that overtook one family. The father was very ill with fever, the mother was blind, and then their baby daughter contracted the fever. The father died, and a barmaid at one of the hessian-sided hotels helped the blind mother to nurse the child. Then the child died. Lonnie heard of the series of calamities and took over arrangements. He made a small coffin out of a condensed milk box and arranged the burial. The procession to the graveside comprised one Salvation Army officer pushing a bicycle on which was a tiny coffin, steadied there by the other officer. Over the coffin was draped a black skirt given by the barmaid. Behind the bicycle walked the blind mother led by the barmaid.[24]

Illness afflicted officers and miners alike. In 1895 women officers were appointed to the goldfields. Many of them acted as nurses to those stricken with typhoid. The work took its toll, however. Cadet-Lieutenant Zilla Smith was sent to Coolgardie early in 1896 to assist Major and Mrs Quick, but became ill after only two weeks and died shortly afterwards.[25] Over her grave are carved the words:

'Away from her home and friends of her youth
She hoisted the standard of mercy and truth,
. . . She died at her post.'[26]

After only eight months at Coolgardie, George Lonnie was promoted to the rank of captain and appointed with only a few days' notice to Wagin Corps in October 1894.[27] Charles Bensley was appointed to divisional headquarters in Adelaide.[28]

Adjutant Charles Bensley eventually returned to Western Australia for further service. Sadly, at the age of only 34, he was promoted to Glory on 31 October 1903 at Northam, Western Australia. A gravestone inscribed 'In loving memory of Adjutant C.H. Bensley' was erected by soldiers and friends of the Northam Corps in the town's cemetery.[29]

CHAPTER 3

Elsewhere in Western and South Australia

Seven months after the move to Wagin, George Lonnie was appointed to the Guildford Corps in Western Australia, effective 4 July 1895.[30] Such rapid changes of appointment were typical in those days as officers were considered to be roving evangelists, although coordinated in their appointments by their leaders.

Thirty-six years later, George told a story from his time in Guilford:

> In the year 1895 I was stationed at Guildford, W.A., and with me was Lieutenant John Powell (now Field-Major R.). Several outposts were worked by us, and one of these was at Bayswater. We had to travel many miles over a dusty, sandy area in those days, to reach the scattered population of this small centre.
>
> When visiting one day we came across a lonely camp in which were two children—a boy of five or six, and a girl much younger.
>
> 'Where is mother, son?' I asked.
>
> 'She is dead, Mister,' he replied.
>
> 'But who looks after you and your sister?'

'Daddy is away all day in the bush, cutting wood. I look after sister, and when dad comes home he cooks tea for us.'

'But are you both alone every day?'

'Yes, Mister.'

My heart went out to the poor father, and I felt that I must try and find him and relieve his burden, and save this dear child from possible harm. Directed by the boy we set off to find him, and before long heard the sound of the axe and discovered the man we were seeking.

We explained why we had sought him, and forthwith he told us his sad story. He had no friends within coo-ee to whom he could turn for help.

'If only I could find a good home for my little girl,' he said wistfully, 'I could struggle on with the boy. I could take him with me to work every day.'

We were deeply moved, and were conscious of the fact that we had been commissioned to bind up the broken-hearted and comfort the sorrowful.

I forthwith asked the father if he would give us his little girl. What a struggle took place then (we had, by this time, returned to the children). The father looked at his darling, and then at me. For some moments not a word was uttered. The children were bewildered. At last, though with tears streaming down his cheeks, the father gave me full possession of his baby girl. And then we knelt and sought the guidance and blessing of our Heavenly Father.

" I FORTHWITH ASKED THE FATHER IF HE WOULD GIVE ME HIS LITTLE GIRL "

The War Cry *artist's 1931 representation of*
Captain George Lonnie and Lieutenant John
Powell trying to arrange alternative and safe
accommodation for the motherless girl.

I took the little one into my arms and tried to win her to
come readily with me. Child-like she agreed to come,
and after kissing her father and brother we set forth. She
held my hand and trotted along quite bravely at first,
but soon the little legs grew weary with trudging in the
heavy sand. For the rest of the way the Lieutenant and
I took turnabout carrying our little treasure. We had to
cross several running streams en route and she made
us to understand she wanted a drink. Having no vessel,
I made a cup out of my hands and held the water to
her lips, and she quenched her thirst. She was as good
as gold all the way home, and when we reached our
quarters we had no difficulty in giving her food and
putting her to sleep, for the long, weary journey had
made her tired and hungry. The neighbours all wondered
what we were doing with so young a child, and it was
quite a novelty for us bachelors to have a tiny toddler in
our quarters.

The next day we had to find a suitable home for our wee friend. My thoughts travelled to our esteemed comrade, recently [probably in about 1930] called Home, Sister Morley of Chiltern Brook 30 miles [48 km] distant. With the wee mite in my arms I set off for Chiltern Brook. No sooner had I explained the circumstances to Sister Morley than this dear comrade took the child to her heart. She was well cared for and grew to be a joy and comfort to Grandma Morley and all with whom she came in contact.[31]

The child he carried through the bush on his shoulders and to whom he gave a drink from a cup made out of his hands when they crossed a creek grew up. Almost 30 years later she made herself known to the then Brigadier George Lonnie when he became the Divisional Commander in Western Australia. By that time, she had made her own decision for Christ, had married, and was the mother of three children of her own. What a happy ending! As George Lonnie wrote:

> Meeting her as I did so many years after, and in such happy circumstances, filled my heart to overflowing, and today my experience with this little girl is among the many happy memories of my officer-career.[32]

From Guildford, George was appointed to Northam in December 1895. He and his lieutenant, Joseph Humbley, had a difficult time there. According to the *Corps Centenary Book 1891–1991*:

> The two officers at the beginning of the year [1896] George Lonnie and Joseph Humbley were having a difficult time with one large lizard that had decided to make its home in the roof of the quarters and continually disturbed them by making a lot of noise. They tried on several occasions to catch the culprit but to no avail. April came and the problem came to a head, the noise had been going on too long. The decision was made to make one last attempt to catch the offender. The attempt began in grand style but my goodness they were in for a shock. From out of its lair

came not only one black angry snake but two and three. The officers were in a state of shock but luckily came to their senses and managed to dispose of the angry snakes with a brick and last of all to catch one large lizard and deposit it far away from their roof. No more noises in the quarter's roof.[33]

Another—probably more significant—story was recorded in 1931 in connection with George Lonnie's retirement. It had to do with a more formidable opponent than the large lizard and three black snakes. A Mr Throssell, who to all intents and purposes 'ran' the town, had been a great supporter of The Salvation Army. However, the Army had been allotted a certain stand for its Saturday night open-air meeting. George was not happy with the location—it did not meet his approval although it had been used by the Corps for some time before his appointment there. He mentioned the fact to the local officers, but they thought it would never do to run counter to the wishes of the leading citizen.

The captain disagreed with his local officers. He announced that next Saturday night the open-air meeting stand would be changed and George formed up his forces right in front of the main door of Mr Throssell's shop. He was immediately called in to see Mr Throssell. This was a situation of 'one strong man against another. At the end of the interview Mr Throssell withdrew whatever support he had previously given to the Army.'[34]

The story did not end there, however. 'One of Mr Throssell's leading foremen had fallen under the power of strong drink. At the time of Captain Lonnie's arrival in town, he was practically incapacitated by debility following excess in drinking.'[35] George was told by one of the foreman's nephews who had become associated with the Army.

George requested to be taken and introduced to the man who was temporally an invalid. In telling the story later, George, then a young man, recalled kneeling down at the side of the chair on which the drunkard sat, 'pleading with him to yield to God, and with God to save such a needy sinner.'[36]

The man surrendered to God and promised that when he was restored to health he would stand in the Army ring and testify. Every day George visited him and gradually his health was restored. When he became well enough to return to work, George kept him to his promise publicly to witness concerning his salvation. George purchased an Army guernsey for him and 'on one memorable night, right in front of Mr Throssell's shop, this one-time drunken foreman stood out—in nervous fear and trembling it must be admitted—and told of God's saving grace.'[37]

> From that day Mr Throssell's attitude changed both to the Army and its captain, who was told that if he ever was in need he must make his wants known without delay. That trophy became one of the Army's most respected Salvationists in the district. One of his daughters became an Army officer, and it is sometimes said that his conversion did more to help forward God's work in the Northam district than any other single factor.[38]

After these adventures and, no doubt, many other good soul-saving efforts in Northam, Captain George Lonnie was appointed to Geraldton for the remainder of the year before an appointment back to the goldfields at Kalgoorlie.

The return of George Lonnie to Kalgoorlie in January 1897 coincided with the completion of a substantial corps hall in the town. Because the contract builder, Mr C. Parker, had made such good progress, the fixing of the memorial (foundation) tablets needed to take place earlier than expected and was arranged rather hurriedly. The official opening of the building by Major Hunter, the Divisional Officer from Perth, took place a month later on 20 February.

According to a report of the laying of the memorial stones of which the author has a copy,

> On Wednesday evening 22nd January about 200 persons assembled in Portman Street in front of the new building— with Captain Lonnie in charge of the proceedings.

Lonnie's name, with that of Bensley and Edmund Ham were well and most favourably known for their early work at Southern Cross and Coolgardie when sickness was so rife; so it was a particularly satisfying occasion for Captain Lonnie to see, now this final building almost completed and requiring the special ceremony of The Tablets. As Lonnie said 'We had no such need at Southern Cross, for the building was run up with poles from the bush; nor later at Coolgardie when the first building was almost as rough; the Salvation Army does not regard Kalgoorlie as something for the present only; it is a real and proper place…'.[39]

That statement was followed by applause.

The building then under construction was 66 feet (20 metre) in length, by 36 feet (11 metre) with a height of 21 feet (6.4 metre); and expected to accommodate 450 persons..[40]

According to a parallel report in the local newspaper, George Lonnie continued that:

… he believed he was right in saying that the building, on the doorway of which he stood, was one of the most substantial in the town. But it was not a building merely for show, but to serve the work for God and for eternity. Nor were the tablets being set merely to pass time, but as an expressive [sic] of their resolve to go on in pointing the way to God. He then called on the Acting Warden, Mr F.R. Bailee to fix up one of the tablets. (Applause.)

Mr Bailee, who was received with prolonged applause, then fixed in its position under the western front window a tablet, coloured in imitation of Aberdeen granite, and bearing the inscription, 'This memorial block was laid to the glory of God by F.R. Bailee, Esq., H.M. Booth, Commandant; Wm. Booth, General'. Addressing the assemblage, Mr Bailee said he declared the block to be well and truly laid to the honor [sic] and glory of God. ('Amen.') As Captain Lonnie had very well said the erection of such a building as this was a monument of the faith held in the future of Kalgoorlie by at least one section of the people. (Applause.) There were, of course, in every community different sections holding diverging views, and though there were some which cavilled at the methods of The Salvation Army, they could not but admit the enthusiasm and enterprise shown by the adherents not only here but throughout the world. It was claimed that the Army was making itself felt everywhere, and that it was a power for good. (Applause.) He congratulated the Army upon possession of the very best building in this town ...

After a hymn, Captain Lonnie made an effective appeal for financial assistance in meeting the big outlay involved in the building of the barracks. Amidst cheers, he announced a donation from Mr W.G. Brookman of 10 guineas, and also, that both Mr Bailee and Mr Hair [who had fixed a second foundation stone under the eastern front window] had promised cheques. The remainder of the time till the dispersal of the gathering was occupied in singing and addresses by the officers. [41]

In order to raise funds to keep the corps operational and to raise more money for the building, George Lonnie and his lieutenant sold multiple copies of *The War Cry*. The circulation rose from 500 to 1,000 during the time, with George and his lieutenant disposing of 830 between them.[42]

George Lonnie's final two appointments in Western Australia at that time were at Perth (September 1897 to August 1898) and Fremantle

(August 1898 to December 1898). The corps history book of Perth Fortress contains the following extract reflecting that period:

> Captain G. Lonnie and Lieutenant Percy 'skippered' the ship from 14.7.97 to 24.8.98. A good dashing officer but had a hard time whilst stationed here owing to the corps being turned out of the old rink, and had to resort to a tent erected on the ground on which the Fortress now stands. Subsequently the old Y.M.C.A. Hall off Hay Street was engaged until the new Fortress was opened. Captain Lonnie had the bulk of the corps amount to raise for the building fund.[43]

The 'old rink' mentioned was Allum's Skating Rink, the first building rented by The Salvation Army in Perth, Western Australia, when it commenced in late 1891. Providentially, the Army purchased land near the corner of Murray and Pier Streets by 1897. When the lease at the rink expired, it was possible to erect a large marquee on the purchased site—until the wind blew it down![44] The Army was then able to secure the services of the Y.M.C.A. Hall while funds were being raised. Having commenced corps in various locations around the State and being an effective fund-raiser, George was ideally suited for the current situation. Construction commenced on the substantial building that was eventually opened in August 1899 after George had been appointed to Fremantle.

George Lonnie's appointment at Fremantle was his shortest in Western Australia, from August 1898 till December that same year. Very little was reported about that time other than the photograph of Captain Lonnie and the Fremantle Juniors—some 12 young ladies with timbrels—in one of The Salvation Army publications, possibly in *The War Cry*. The story about a decade later indicated that nine candidates offered for officership during his term at Fremantle, three of whom became adjutants by1910, namely Adjutants Bailey, Munro and Scott.[45] So George could not only plant corps and raise finances, he could also raise up and inspire potential leaders.

In December 1898, George was appointed in charge of Adelaide Corps in South Australia, being promoted to the rank of Ensign in

February 1899. An old photograph dated 1897 (although erroneously labelled Ensign G. Lonnie) shows him with a bicycle such as he would have used to 'move around among the people' or transport the child's coffin on the goldfields.

Captain George Lonnie and his bicycle, c. 1897.

Whilst in Adelaide, he had a team of 12 *War Cry* boomers (sellers) plus himself, which was able to distribute 630 copies a week—a rise of 30 per week to the year before. They always commenced the distribution with a song and prayers before getting on with the business. So, although necessary funds were raised for the corps by their efforts, they saw this as a spiritual exercise.

Adelaide War Cry boomers (sellers),
The War Cry *6 May 1899.*

After seven months at Adelaide, George was transferred to Norwood in July 1899 and continued there until April 1900. One recorded feature of his time at Norwood was the fact that he was able to secure the services of the Melbourne Headquarters Band for a Saturday and Sunday at his corps during the visit of General Booth to Adelaide. The Sunday night meeting was led by Colonel John Lawley.[46]

During that time in South Australia, the 'dashing' George Lonnie met the young woman for whom he had unknowingly collected the specks of gold at Fly Creek, Western Australia, namely Jennie Hammer.

CHAPTER 4

The children's worker from Ballarat

Like the Lonnie (or Lonie) and the McCarter (or McCarty) families, the Hammer and Brokenshire families also came to Victoria seeking gold. It appears that the father of the Hammer family, 29-year-old William, arrived in June 1854. He was followed two years later by his then 34-year-old wife Maria and eight small children including 14-year-old Richard.[47] They had come from Saint Austell, Cornwall, England. Richard eventually became a goldminer.[48]

Similarly, James and Elizabeth Brokenshire arrived in Victoria in 1857 and moved to Ballarat from Dudley, West Midlands. They brought with them from England three children including the then 16-year-old Annie (Ann or Anne) Brokenshire.[49]

Richard Hammer and Annie Brokenshire married in 1865 and subsequently had 13 children, all born in Ballarat, Victoria. Five of these children died before they were five years of age. The oldest surviving child was Mary Jane Hammer who was born on 2 March 1870, a few months before an older brother died at the age of four. [50]

Being the eldest in the family, Mary Jane was given the opportunity for all the basic education that was possible in those days—primary school and some secondary schooling until she was about the age of 14. Hers was a Christian home in which her parents attended the Wesleyan church and the children were encouraged to attend both church and Sunday school and study the Bible. However, Mary Jane drifted away from Sunday school and the church at one stage. She really tried to believe there was no God. ... 'But one day, whilst looking through a microscope at the beauty of a marguerite daisy, I felt there must be a God, yet I continue to follow the pleasures and fashions of the world, and pride and self-will filled my heart,' she recorded many years later.[51]

Mary Jane changed her name to Jennie sometime before turning 26, because all Salvation Army records indicate her name as Jennie (or Jeannie) Hammer.

The Salvation Army was already making its presence felt in Ballarat with work having commenced about the middle of February 1883.[52] In 1891, seven women officers were in five groups of Salvationists who suffered imprisonment for marching in Sturt Street in the city. The mayor of Ballarat, Mayor Shoppe, was opposed to the methods of The Salvation Army. In fact, Mayor Shoppe tried to stop General William Booth from visiting the city as the Founder travelled from Adelaide to Melbourne in 1895. Apparently, the Mayor replied to a request for official permission for the General to hold meetings in Ballarat and stay overnight as follows: 'I have made a search of the military list but failed to discover any name such as that mentioned, and therefore permission cannot be granted.' Fortunately, wisdom prevailed and some 600 Salvationists and a number of Salvation Army bands marched along the route to the Albert Hall through portion of the West Municipality of Ballarat.[53]

However, the persecutions and prosecutions continued. In February 1892, seven officers and soldiers were charged with street marching and fined £5 ($10) each with costs or, in default, one month's imprisonment. All seven served the full sentences. Apparently, many citizens of Ballarat were incensed at this. Bishop Thornton headed a deputation of protest to the Mayor, and ultimately restrictions on the Army marching were removed, and a fifth group then imprisoned were released by order of the Executive Council of Victoria.[54]

We do not know how the Hammer family responded to these events. Certainly their 22-year-old daughter, Jennie, could not have failed to appreciate what was going on. She initially had 'no time for the Army', but God had other plans. Years later, she recorded how these unfolded:

One day I heard that a Salvation Army officer had come to Ballarat East Corps,[55] and whilst I had no time for the Army, it had been stated in the town that this new officer had said to his soldiers one Sunday night, 'Go home and pray. I won't waste gas on you. You will never get sinners saved unless you are right yourselves.'

The local people were very angry. How dare he talk to Ballarat people like that? Interest was aroused, and out of curiosity I went with others to see this man. I went on three Sunday evenings, but would not go during the week, for I feared to come too close to these people. It was a new thing for me to see people coming forward for salvation.

I was not asked to be saved until one evening Sergeant-Major Monod (father of Mrs Colonel Suttor R.) dealt with me. I was convicted of sin, but I knew my whole life would have to be altered. I was not willing to pay the price. I tried to leave the hall, but was too afraid, so finally I came to the mercy seat at 11:15 pm, on 21 August 1896. I took one week to decide whether I would link up with the Army or the Church, but during that week I got rid of all my outward adorning so that it would be hard for me to retrace my steps, for I knew too well my own weaknesses.

When I decided to join the Army, the new Ensign gave me work to do at once amongst the young people, and afterwards I became the Young People's Sergeant-Major. I was not allowed to wear uniform, for my folk resented me joining the Army. I was offered a new outfit as a tempting bait to go to church, and for six weeks I held out against this offer, but one day in a fit of temper I said words which afterwards I regretted. I immediately saw how frail my own will was, so that night in the Young People's Hall I attended the holiness meeting and publicly confessed my wrong.

I was very nervous over my confession because the Ensign had just made a comrade sit down because he did not think he had lived right; but at last I said, 'Ensign, may I speak?'

'Yes,' he answered.

I then made my confession and that night received the blessing of Holiness.[56]

Young People's Sergeant Major Jennie Hammer, 1896.

God had other things to say to Jennie Hammer as well. One was on the matter of humility in regard to success in spiritual things and another about officership. She continued,

At the end of three months the officer asked for recent converts to stand, and, as 23 of us—mostly young men and women—stood, to our amazement Ensign cried, 'God, forgive me for this sin, numbering the people for my own glory. God forgive me!' I shall never forget that night.

As the time came for the Ensign to farewell, I made a bargain with God regarding officership. I did not want to leave the corps but I knew that if the Ensign spoke to me about officership this was the sign that God had directed his words. At the conclusion of the meeting, I said good-bye to him, and was leaving the hall—glad to get away—when he called me back and said, 'God wants you; I'll hear of you again.' This convinced me of the way which I should take.[57]

Obedient to God's call, Jennie applied to become an officer in October 1897 and received notification of acceptance for training in December. She entered the Training Home in June the following year. In September 1898 she was made a Cadet Lieutenant and appointed as Assistant at Hope Hall Women's Shelter and Slum Post, Melbourne. She was promoted to the rank of Lieutenant on 28 October 1898, before being appointed in charge of the Adelaide Women's Rescue Home, in South Australia in November. Almost 30 years later she recalled that, with her companion lieutenant, she knelt in the train and asked God to give them a message from his Word. The message they read was, 'Thy shoes shall be iron and brass, and as thy days so shall thy strength be' (Deuteronomy 33:25 KJV).[58]

For her New Year motto in 1899, Jennie chose the text, 'That in all things He might have the pre-eminence' (Colossians 1:18 KJV). Some 28 years later she reported that this text had continued to be her slogan ever since.[59]

Promoted to the rank of Captain in May 1899, Jennie was appointed to pioneer the Adelaide Women's Shelter (Slum Work) in July prior to a pro tem appointment at Adelaide Maternity Home in September. A matter of weeks later she was appointed to the Rescue Sisters Home, Adelaide, where she stayed for three months.

*Adelaide Slum Sisters, 1899. Jennie
Hammer is second from the left.*

During that frantically busy year of 1899, caring for women involved in prostitution and working to alleviate the needs of poverty-struck people around the slums of Adelaide, Jennie met the 'dashing' Ensign George Lonnie who was successively in charge at Adelaide and Norwood Corps. George himself must have been impressed by the intelligent, articulate and dedicated Captain Jennie Hammer who could be an 'ideal counterpart to his rugged, virile personality.'[60]

As good and loyal Salvation Army officers, George and Jennie would have expressed the desire to 'correspond with a view to marriage'. The Army's response was to appoint Jennie as the Matron of Hope Hall Women's Shelter and Slum Post, in Little Bourke Street, Melbourne in January 1900, and George to Charters Towers in Queensland in April the same year! Undeterred, the couple continued to develop their relationship by correspondence, leading to Jennie accepting George's proposal of marriage sometime that year. No doubt a jeweller in Charters Towers fashioned the gold that George had collected at Fly Creek in 1894 into a broad wedding band for his beloved.

During the final four months before their marriage in January 1901, Jennie served as Grace Before Meat (GBM) Special Officer, Victoria, at the Men's Social Office. In this role, Jennie moved from place to place around Victoria bringing first-hand accounts of the social service work being undertaken amongst the needy people by The Salvation Army. The stories encouraged people to provide a helping hand financially toward the less fortunate. The GBM scheme provided families with a small money box that could be placed on the meal table into which those present could place a small coin, ideally not less than one penny per week, as a practical token of gratitude for their own meals. Such small amounts collected from across all the colonies (now states of the Commonwealth) would help to fund the social services work of the movement.[61] According to the advertised itinerary in *The War Cry*, we know Jennie visited several centres in Gippsland, Victoria, during those months.

Just four years had passed since that conversation with the Ensign at Ballarat East at which Jennie was challenged about officership and now she was due to travel to Brisbane to marry George Lonnie. Learning that Adjutant Walls—he was 'the Ensign'—was in Melbourne and very ill, Jennie called on him. She wrote that she would never forget his words and his charge to her as she knelt at his bedside. 'Be faithful to God and the Army. If you ever hear anyone say that Army work killed me tell them this is untrue. I am dying for the sins of my youth.'[62]

Jennie continued: 'Soon after this he went to New Zealand, and shortly afterwards was promoted to Glory. It was definitely the influence of this godly man which led to my conversion and ultimate officership.'[63]

The wedding of Ensign George Lonnie and Captain Jennie Hammer took place in the Brisbane Temple on Thursday night, 31 January 1901. *The War Cry* report indicates that:

> The date was most fitting, being the eighth anniversary of the Ensign's officership. The ceremony was conducted by our State leader, Brigadier Bruntnell. There was a large number of staff, field and social officers present. Both our comrades are well known. The Ensign's last command was Charters Towers and, judging by the telegraphic expressions of good wishes he received from the corps, he has left a good and lasting impression there. Captain Hammer has been very successful as a slum officer in Adelaide and Melbourne, and recently in an important position as a G.B.M. special to

the state of Victoria. Ensign Lonnie is fortunate in securing such a wife. The ceremony has gone through with much precision. The 'I wills' were heard in advantage, and in each case were very emphatic. The Brigadier then read a large budget of telegrams from every state in the Commonwealth, after which some comrade officers arose and spoke of what they personally knew of the godly character of the bride and bridegroom. The Brigadier then made a few lucid remarks on the career of our comrades. He had no hesitation in predicting a term of successful blessing for them at Brisbane 1. Ensign Lonnie described how God had led him up to the present, his determination to be true, and concluded by saying, 'I have the best wife in the world'. Mrs Lonnie was enthusiastically received. She made a most interesting speech and stated that she felt God had led her in this matter. She also expressed her love for the fight, and her desire, to win victories for God and the Army.[64]

Wedding photograph of George and Jennie, January 1901.

Thus the former carpenter from Yackandandah and the former children's worker from Ballarat came together in service for God with their first united appointment at Brisbane Temple.

They served at Brisbane 1 for almost 12 months before being appointed to Ipswich in January 1902. After six months there, George suffered a health collapse and was compelled to go on five-month rest in Victoria. Then from November 1902 until April 1904 they were appointed back to Queensland, this time to Toowoomba with the rank of Adjutant.[65] During those years Ivy Isabel Lonnie was born on 5 April 1902 and Harry Vaughan Lonnie on 12 November 1903.

CHAPTER 5

New Zealand

Except for a brief period from 1889 to 1894, Salvation Army work in New Zealand was officially part of the Australasian Territory from 1882 until 1912.[66] Officers could be easily transferred from one country to another during those years at the decision of the Territorial Commander based in Melbourne, Australia.

Auckland

'Farewell orders came just as we were going into our soldiers' meeting,' wrote Jennie Lonnie in a *War Cry* article headed 'To Cooler Climes' in 1904. '*"Proceed to New Zealand!"* caused quite a thrill, while I must confess my heart sank at the prospect of a sea trip with my bairns. Still, we must obey!'[67] Jennie went on to recount their farewell, train journey to Sydney and then a very rough sea voyage on the SS *Mokoia* to Auckland during which George was the victim of seasickness.

So it was that the now Adjutants George and Mrs Jennie Lonnie, together with their two children, Ivy and Harry, moved from Toowoomba, Queensland to the Auckland Corps in New Zealand between April 1904 and January 1905. They were warmly welcomed, with 20 of their comrades reconsecrating themselves for service during their welcome Sunday morning meeting, and five seekers for salvation in the night meeting.[68] From a photograph in the Australian

War Cry 18 June 1904, some other Australian officers were also appointed to Auckland at that time including Lieutenant S. Botheras and Candidate F. Arnel.

Captain Mary Anderson, a New Zealand officer, born in Akaroa in 1875, but from Oamaru Corps, New Zealand, in the province of Christchurch, trained as an officer in Melbourne during 1901. By all reports, Mary was small in appearance and timid. She was not commissioned with others in her session, but eventually served at seven corps in Victoria and New South Wales until her appointment to the Auckland Rescue Home in 1904. In July that year she was appointed to the Auckland Corps to assist Adjutants George and Mrs Jennie Lonnie. This was a mutually beneficial arrangement as Mary Anderson was able to give good support to the Lonnies and their young family and also learnt much about enthusiastic Salvationism and caring for the needy.

Adjutant and Mrs Lonnie with Captain
Mary Anderson (centre).

As already mentioned, corps appointments for officers were generally short in those days. On Sunday, 15 January 1905, the Lonnies and Captain Anderson were farewelled from Auckland Corps. They anticipated commencing the 580 nautical mile (930 km) journey by sea to Port Lyttelton, the harbour nearest to their next appointment at Christchurch in the South Island, on Tuesday 17th. On arriving home on the Sunday night, however, they found that Harry was unwell. The next day the doctor diagnosed 'double pneumonia' and held out no hope for his recovery. Antibiotics such as penicillin were not available in those days. Mary Anderson recorded that for the next five weeks his parents 'faithfully watched and nursed him.'[69] Although the service record for the Lonnies shows them leaving the Auckland appointment on 19 January 1905, the Army's Archives in New Zealand has recently found the register showing officers at Auckland that has them leaving their appointment 9 March 1905 and Mary Anderson leaving the Auckland appointment on the same date.[70] So their departure was delayed for the sake of their ailing child and it was in Auckland that 15-month-old Harry died in his mother's arms on 17 February. His funeral was conducted the next day by Staff-Captain Bishop.[71]

The Melbourne *War Cry*, 25 February 1905, relates how a cablegram had been received from Adjutant Lonnie the week before, containing just four simple words: 'Our boy died today'. The report continued, 'In this terse sentence is embodied a whole volume of grief and sorrow for a loss that cannot be remedied. Those who have suffered a similar affliction will realise what it means to the sorrowing parents. They have the fullest sympathy of their comrades everywhere. Pray that sustaining grace may be given to them in this hour of trial.'[72]

Frank Woodroffe in *The War Cry*, New Zealand, 4 March 1905, having reported Harry's death 'after nearly five weeks of suffering' concludes his article referring to George and Jennie: 'They have the deepest sympathy and prayers of their many Auckland friends as they leave Auckland for Christchurch in a few days.'[73]

Christchurch

God answered those faithful prayers from both sides of the Tasman Sea for George, Jennie and little Ivy. The appointment at Christchurch, which continued until March 1907, was one of much blessing but many challenges.

On the family front, the safe arrival on 8 June 1905 of Florence Burgess Lonnie, who eventually became my mother, would have been a great blessing, and helped to relieve something of the grief of the death of little Harry earlier in the year.

Nevertheless, and quite understandably, as well as helping Ivy face normal childhood fears, Jennie and George would have needed to help her deal with the grief of losing her young brother and the fear that she too might die. In an article published in *The War Cry,* New Zealand edition, later that year, headed 'Why Do the Shadows Come?', Jennie wrote as follows:

> 'I'm so frightened, Mamma!', said three-year-old Ivy, as her blue eyes filled with tears and her little lip quivered.

> 'Nothing can hurt you, my darling,' replied her mother, and tried to soothe the fears away. 'Tell me what you are afraid of.'

> But the child was unable to put into words the fears that haunted her.

> 'I'm afraid of something,' she whispered.

> That night, as she said her prayers, her mother encouraged her to put in an extra petition: 'Please, Jesus, do take care of Ivy tonight.' Very earnestly were these words uttered. The cloud for a little time was lifted, as her mother said: 'You belong to Jesus; he will take care of you. Jesus watches all night; he never sleeps.'

> Ivy has always been afraid of dogs, big or small. A tiny dog was enough to cause hours of wakefulness. While she lay in her bed, the active little brain would credit the animal with all kinds of powers. Next day, when she was out walking, and a dog came running up to her, instead

of shrinking away in terror, she shook her tiny head, and said, very decidedly: –'You can't hurt me; I'm the Lord's.'

However, that night the little heart was very fearful. Undressed and ready for bed, she had finished her prayers and risen to her feet, when, to her mother's surprise, she dropped on her knees, and closing her eyes and clasping her hands, said: 'Please, Jesus, don't let Ivy be frightened.' After tucking her in her tiny cot that night, her mother lingered about the room, intending to remain until the blue eyes had closed in sleep. For a few minutes Ivy laid quite quiet, watching the shadow thrown on the wall from the canopy of her cot, and then said: – 'Mamma, I don't like shadows.'

And the nervous little girl conjured up faces and all manner of terrors out of the shadows. Her mother talked, tried to reason her out of her fears, showed her how simply the shadows came, and how we could make our own.

'Mamma, I belong to the Lord, don't I?' asked the child again.

'Yes, dear,' answered her mother.

'Well, if I belong to the Lord, why do the shadows come? They frightened me.'

Dear comrades, this is a question which our hearts, if not our voices, often ask. We know and realise that we belong to the Lord; still, we don't know and we don't understand why the shadows come. Just as the knowledge comforted little Ivy, so it can be of help and blessing to us to know that Jesus always takes care of us.

'Tell Jesus all about the troubles
That on your life do press;
For in him dwells all the love and power

To make the pressure less —
Only tell him.'[74]

Among the other blessings of their appointment in Christchurch was the fact that 19 new soldiers were sworn in by Adjutant Lonnie in July 1905. H. Bramwell Cook relates that the period between a person kneeling in confession and being sworn in as a soldier was comparatively short—three weeks in 1899 and about eight weeks in 1905. Thirteen names of the 19 were removed from the soldiers roll for backsliding, nine within two years and another four within five years. Cook believed that: 'The gospel preached was simple, clearly stated and unambiguous, and the sincerity of the officers was not in doubt.' He goes on to raise significant questions as to whether many of these new converts had sufficient time to resolve in their own minds the place of God in their lives, or whether these raw soldiers had not been tenderly and sufficiently nurtured after the excitement of their first experiences.[75]

According to Cook, back in 1888, a Christchurch Lasses Band made its first public appearance in an open-air meeting and apparently added much vibrancy to corps meetings for a number of years. Sadly, this initial lasses band lost its enthusiasm before the turn of the century. Having encouraged brass bands in Australia, George Lonnie had the Lasses Band re-formed in 1905 under the leadership of Bandmaster Tom Young. 'The girls take part in open-airs weekly, also contributing good music indoors,' related a report in *The War Cry*.[76] In 1906, the Christchurch bandsmen were also fitted out with new red tunics in time for the Exhibition Congress of February 1907. Their tunics were the same design chosen for the lasses band earlier and the men also managed to raise enough money to purchase a new set of instruments.[77]

Christchurch Corps Lasses Band c. 1905 with
Adjutant Lonnie and Bandmaster Tom Young.

When it came to fundraising, George continued the good work he had commenced in his homeland. As Cook records, 'The annual Self-Denial Appeal, usually in the month of October, placed a heavy burden on corps officers, who strive to visit every household in the district.'[78] Believing in delegation and providing good leadership, *The War Cry*, 25 November 1905, reported that:

> Early in September, Adjutant Lonnie called together eight
> of the leading soldiers of the Christchurch Corps, and laid
> before them his plans for the coming Self-Denial Appeal.
> Each one was entrusted with a fair portion of the City, also
> a good staff of working soldiers, who gave a satisfactory
> account of themselves at the end of the Appeal.[79]

Cook indicates that Adjutant George Lonnie collected £120 (equivalent to NZ$16,500 in 2008) and Captain Mary Anderson £53.3.4 ($7,312.25) that year. 'Their total was the highest ever collected by any two officers at this corps for one Appeal.' Seven seekers were recorded during the Altar Service at the conclusion of the Appeal with numbers of soldiers testifying to the blessings they received by being involved.[80] While the headline of the same *War Cry* article announced that a total of 26 seekers were recorded and 430 sovereigns (£451 or $62,102.50) collected during the Appeal, the final paragraph of the report indicates the total money raised was £430 ($59,125)—nevertheless an increase of £30 ($4,125) over the previous year.[81]

The following year the corps' target for the Appeal was £400. Using a similar approach augmented by efforts from some of the Army's social service centres in Christchurch, the corps raised £501, including £56.08.11 from the young people's corps. George personally collected £137.08.6 and Jennie Lonnie £13.03.3. The now Ensign Mary Anderson, who was injured in a fall on the third day of the collection, raised £5.06.6. Even the Lonnies' now four-and-a-half-year-old daughter Ivy managed to collect £2.11.2.[82] She was being trained early!

Earlier in 1906 great emphasis was placed on the annual Harvest Festival celebrations. From 20 March the two bands and singing company from Christchurch Citadel supported other corps in the area such as Sydenham and Linwood with their efforts to raise funds while celebrating God's goodness. After that the focus was on Christchurch's celebrations. Much effort was put into decorating the Citadel with fruit and vegetables together with oats, wheat, evergreens and scenery. For the Saturday night programme, 'the Band Lasses turned out in harvest costume with aprons and big straw hats neatly trimmed with oats, wheat and poppies, while the band lads turned out in costumes to suit the occasion.'[83] After the Sunday meetings the produce given by kind friends was sold. Many corps members participated in making this a very worthy occasion.

A *War Cry* report in April 1906 recorded that the Christchurch Citadel Corps had 200 soldiers and recruits on the roll with the corps being well organised. No fewer than 74 local officers were in active service, including two fine bands. As recently as a week before the report, 15 more new soldiers were enrolled.[84]

After two successful years at Christchurch, George and Jennie together with Mary Anderson received farewell orders to move to

Dunedin City Corps. The newly-promoted Staff-Captain George Lonnie would also have responsibility for the Dunedin Division. As they farewelled, Jennie wrote an article summarising their time at Christchurch.

> God has truly been with us. Evidences of this are seen on our platform, in soldiers and bandsman made out of penitents who have sought and found mercy. Finance has gone up by leaps and bounds. Treasurer Melville aptly puts it: 'Adjutant Lonnie can get the cash easier than any officer I have met.' The corps also occupies premier position in the Colony for WAR CRY sales. The band was never in a better position and is having a fine opportunity under the tuition of Captain Sutton. The Lasses' Band—God bless them!—have been of untold help and blessing to the officers, especially on Monday nights and the soldiers generally are in good fighting trim.
>
> Nearly every Junior on the roll attends each Sunday. Envoy Dawson has the work well in hand, and is helped by a staff of locals. The writer spent 14 months with the Young People, and has tried hard to win the first class [specifically] of boys for the Master. A Bible Class for girls was inaugurated with the Y.P. Campaign, and the interest and attendance are well sustained...
>
> Our farewell meetings were of the right character; the crowds being good, especially at night, when the leading local officers expressed their regret at parting with us, and prayed God's blessing on the departing officers. Special reference was made to the thoroughness of the Adjutant's work from those who were most closely associated with him. Our last soldiers' meeting was attended by nearly 100 soldiers. Songs were sung and each part of the corps was represented. Captain Prowse farewelled for Linwood. Captain Anderson, with tears streaming down her face, thanked all who had been so kind to her during her accident. The Adjutant's last words to the soldiers were

full of blessing, and we believe will help in the future. We treasure very much the token of love given by the soldiers to Ivy and Florrie. — J.L.[85]

Dunedin City Corps and Division

The only significant highlights I could discover about the Lonnies' 14 months of service in Dunedin were about music and song.

The first was about the advent of the Miriamites—the Dunedin City Corps Timbrel Brigade. No doubt the name of the group came about because of the actions of Miriam, sister of Moses and Aaron, after the children of Israel had successfully crossed the Red Sea and the Egyptian army had been destroyed trying to follow them. 'Then Miriam the prophetess, Aaron's sister, took a tambourine in her hand, and all the women followed her, with tambourines and dancing. Miriam sang to them: "Sing to the Lord, for he is highly exalted. The horse and its rider he has hurled into the sea"' (Exodus 15:20–21). Supported by the corps band, the Miriamites 'having wheeled here and there through the main streets, duly made their appearance before a large crowd.' All 13 of them were very active in presenting a programme of some 14 items. Recitations, songs and solos were featured. As a *War Cry* report continued, 'every item was of a salvation character' and George Lonnie made a spiritual appeal based on one of the choruses they sang, 'Some mother's girl'. The Miriamites' final song, 'Bring the crowd to the Cross' summed up their mission and purpose.[86]

Six months later, George was active in promoting a scheme to make the Army's message clearly known in Dunedin:

> Staff-Captain Lonnie has launched a scheme in the City of Dunedin, N.Z., with a view to raising 150 pounds to help purchase of a new set of Class A Triumph instruments. It is twenty-five years come April 1st since the first shot was fired at the historic Fountain, and the Dunedinites have decided that the scheme for the purchase new instruments is a fitting way to celebrate their semi-jubilee.[87]

Meanwhile, on Boxing Day 1907, Jennie received a cable, 'Mother at rest,' informing her that her mother, Mrs Anne Hammer, had been released from her suffering and gone home to be with her Lord at 58 years of age. From her youth and early years, Mrs Hammer was associated with the Wesleyan Church in Ballarat, Victoria. Plans were being developed for Jennie to visit Ballarat to receive her mother's final blessing, 'but God knew best. The silver cord was loosed, and mother and daughter will meet in the realms of the blest,' wrote Captain Mary Anderson.[88] Jennie was able to take three months furlough in mid-1908, probably to return to Ballarat to sort out family affairs following the death of her mother.[89]

Wellington City Corps and Division

Staff-Captain George and Mrs Jennie Lonnie served with Captain Mary Anderson as their assistant at Wellington City Corps and Wellington Division from April 1908 to February 1910. They were welcomed to the corps on Easter Sunday night by a crowd of 600 people. Both Jennie and George spoke of their love for God and desire to lead others to find him—and there were three seekers at the conclusion of the meeting. At a variety of indoor and open-air meetings a further 30 souls sought the Lord in the first week of their ministry. H.F. McKenzie, the writer of *The War Cry* report, concluded 'Our hopes are high for the future. Our motto is, "Wellington for God!"'[90]

Lieutenant Ernest Kemp, George Lonnie's nephew, the son of Charlotte Kemp (nee Lonnie) had been a soldier of the Brunswick Corps, Victoria, before becoming an officer. His first appointment was to Invercargill Corps in New Zealand in September 1907. From there he was appointed to assist George at Wellington Corps from June 18 1908 until April 1910.[91]

Having encouraged the lasses band in Christchurch, George and Jennie would have been delighted to have a similar group of female musicians supporting the work of the corps at Wellington.[92]

With his enthusiasm for *War Cry* sales in all his previous appointments, George had an early meeting with the Wellington *War Cry* boomers (sellers). They not only distributed copies of the publication around Wellington but also took them into the developing suburb of Brooklyn which then had a population of 3,400 people. This district had recently been transferred to the command of the City Corps from Newtown Corps.[93] The Wellington City Corps Band supported these efforts by conducting open-air witnessing in and around Brooklyn in August and September 1908.[94]

Throughout the time that George and Jennie, together with Mary Anderson and Ernest Kemp, led the Wellington Corps, the officers emphasised holiness teaching in holiness and soldiers meetings. Many comrades made recommitments to the Lord or sought the blessing of holiness during those months. A significant spiritual breakthrough took place in a soldiers meeting in September 1908. As *War Cry* reporter 'H.F.' (perhaps H.K. McKenzie) noted, those present felt that they were on holy ground.

> The Staff-Captain [George Lonnie] asked all those who were really anxious to seek a closer walk with God, and who were prepared to abandon themselves completely to His will, to stand their feet and make a definite consecration. A subdued stillness pervaded the meeting, which was broken by comrades rising to their feet as with uplifted, tear-stained faces they prayed to God to accept their humble offering. Over 60 took this step. Following this definite act came the most hallowed spiritual season in the writer's experience. Truly, our hearts were stirred by the Holy Ghost. The prayers were not stereotyped phrases but simple human heart-cries to God. A number who hitherto had been afraid to pray in public claimed that perfect love that casts out fear. Songs, cries and tears mingled with shouts of praise. One brother thanked God for the baptism of the Holy Ghost. Another prayed for an increase of faith; and a sister, between her sobs, cried 'O God, sanctify me now.' Yet another prayed, 'Lord help me

> to demonstrate Thy power among the people with whom
> I live.' Staff-Captain Lonnie testified that he had never
> before experienced God's presence so near him and his
> love so precious as he did in this meeting. We were loath
> to close, though over two hours had gone. It was a prayer-
> meeting from beginning to end, and all other business was
> suspended.[95]

In his concurrent appointment as Divisional Officer, George encouraged every corps to work hard to raise their annual Self Denial Appeal targets in 1908. The divisional target was £1,286 and the amount eventually raised by the seven corps in the district was £1,871—an increase of £585.[96]

Jennie Lonnie was delighted to report on the success of the Young Peoples Annual (Anniversary) at Wellington in 1909 led by Staff-Captain Orames. The (Sunday school) 'children and [Company] Guards occupied the platform for the afternoon and night meetings. An orchestra of 15, including five violinists from the Y.P. Corps gave efficient service all through the series of meetings.' Young People's Sergeant-Major Lankshear was congratulated on the fact that he and his 12 company guards (teachers) had 107 children on the roll with average attendance of 99. Of particular interest was a feature in the Sunday night meeting in which 'testimonies were asked for and given by those who were converted when under 15 years of age. Fifty-three stood to their feet, acknowledging the fact that God can save and keep the children.'[97]

George and Jennie highly esteemed the Lord's day. A weekend roast (if the family could afford it) was prepared and sometimes eaten on Saturday rather than on a busy Salvation Army Sunday. Housework was kept to a minimum. Ivy and Florrie early learned that shoes to be worn on Sunday were to be cleaned no later than Saturday night—habits they carried through into their adult lives and taught their children.

I can remember my mother, Florrie, who was born in Christchurch in 1905, frequently testified in later years that she made her decision for Christ as a four-year-old (about 1909) at her mother's knee. This must have taken place at Wellington.

In early 1910, the Lonnies' service in New Zealand concluded. Together with the newly promoted Ensign Mary Anderson, they were appointed to Sydney, New South Wales, with George in charge of the Sydney 1 Corps.

Florence (left) and Ivy Lonnie (right) c. 1910.

CHAPTER 6

Back in Australia – Sydney and Brisbane

The Lonnies' appointment at Sydney City from February 1910 till December 1912, with Ensign Mary Anderson, brought with it many joys and some sorrows.

One of those joys was George's opportunity to take a furlough in Melbourne with his relatives, presumably the Kemps, who resided in Brunswick, Victoria. The visit coincided with a campaign by Colonel Samuel Logan Brengle, a renowned international preacher and teacher of Christian holiness, at Brunswick Corps. George relished the meetings and took every opportunity to move around the congregation during the prayer meeting after Brengle's addresses, encouraging people to respond and make commitment to living a life of holiness.[98] That probably explains why my mother inherited several personally autographed copies of some of Brengle's books on holiness.

As he had at other corps in Australia and New Zealand, George quickly recruited a team of *War Cry* sellers to take the publication around the streets and into public houses to raise money for the corps and to share the gospel. A photograph in the 22 October 1910 *War Cry*, showed a team of 36 enthusiastic brigade members for Sydney 1 Corps, including the corps officers, Staff-Captain and Mrs Lonnie and Ensign Anderson. Captain Knight, Captain Magill and Adjutant Harper were also officer-members of the team. Whether they were the assistant officers or simply officer-soldiers in headquarters or social services appointments is hard to determine at this point of time.[99] The corps' regular order for *The War Cry* in 1910 was 450. During the Easter period in 1911, the brigade sold 2,222 copies of the Easter edition of *The War Cry,* with 1,111 copies now being their usual weekly order.[100] In faith, George ordered 3,000 copies of the Christmas *War Cry* that year.[101]

The extra money was essential because the original Sydney City Temple was to be demolished, the last meeting being held on 22 June 1911.[102] From that point the corps had to meet in a tent until the new building was constructed and officially opened. Of course, George was used to such situations. He had pioneered corps in challenging situations on the Western Australian goldfields and a tent had been needed for meetings in Perth when he was the corps officer there in 1897.

To compound the difficulties, the Sydney Municipal Council had enacted regulations prohibiting mass meetings in the streets. By and large, the local newspapers such as the *The Sydney Morning Herald* were warmly positive about giving The Salvation Army the opportunity of ministering on the streets as a 'moral right to special consideration'. One editorial continued,

> To put it succinctly, to sweep the little gatherings of philanthropic enthusiasts off the streets is practically to paralyse an admittedly most useful organisation. The whole rationale of The Salvation Army's existence is founded on its mission to the man in the street. Its most conspicuous trophies had been gathered from the outer circumference of the 'ring.' Its work has been so largely centred upon the attractions of its public appearances that the street meeting is vital to its presence in the city as a philanthropic and moral force. In this it stands apart from the other branches of the Christian Church, for, although the churches have often adopted Army methods, their main work lies, so to speak, within doors and their services are, as everyone knows, conducted in buildings devoted to that purpose.[103]

Commissioner James Hay assisted by Mrs Hay opened Sydney's new Temple early in February 1912. The magnificent building was designed by Lieut-Colonel Edward Saunders, one of the pioneers of The Salvation Army in Australia, based on suggestions by the Territorial Commander, and confirmed by the Colonel's detailed knowledge reported in *The War Cry* 17 February 1912. He had been in charge of the Army's Property Department from 1889. Lieut-Colonel Saunders commented to the *War Cry* reporter at the time, 'Now I am satisfied. I have tried to carry out the Commissioner's suggestions. I have tried to embody in bricks and mortar all he has wished, and I now see that this is not only a question of so much material, but we have erected a Temple to the living God.'[104]

As part of the opening ceremony, Commissioner Hay dedicated George Sydney Lonnie, the infant son of George and Jennie, who had been born on 23 December 1911. Sadly, the boy died on 25 February 1912—a few weeks after his dedication. Following the death of little Harry seven years before, George Sydney's passing was another grief for these dedicated officers in the middle of all the relief and joy of the new building being opened. Many messages of sympathy were directed toward George, Jennie and their children at that time. And George responded, 'Sometime we'll understand, we know "His way is perfect," and we'll trust Him.'[105] Reflecting on the event later in 1912, Jennie wrote an article for the Christmas edition of *The War Cry* about Florrie's great faith back in 1911 that a boy would be born. Apparently, Ivy and Florrie had saved up pennies and halfpennies so that Father Christmas would give them something special that year. What a delight for them when George Sydney was born just two days before Christmas! Ivy and Florrie prayed, 'Thank you, Jesus, we'll teach him to be good.' But then, just nine short weeks later, their baby brother had gone to be with Jesus, too. In the midst of her own grief and questioning, six-year-old Florrie tried to comfort her mother as best she could, and was heard to pray at her bedside: 'Please, Jesus, if you could spare us another baby, would you send it to our house, but give it to us to keep this time, not just for a lend; we'll teach him to be good.'[106]

As elsewhere, George and Jennie were concerned to build up the numbers of Army officer personnel as well as encouraging developments of buildings. They had at least 12 candidates for officership from the Sydney 1 Corps by October 1911, seven women and three men.[107]

Candidates from Sydney 1 Corps in 1911,
with Staff-Captain George Lonnie.

A report covering the six months to March 1912 was full of rejoicing—despite the challenges of the four months during which their meetings needed to be held in a tent. Theirs was the first corps in the Commonwealth to bring in more than £1,000 for the Self Denial Appeal. Seekers for salvation totalled 198, with a number of others seeking holiness of heart. Thirty new soldiers were added to the soldiers roll together with a large number of recruits awaiting enrolment. Four candidates had been sent to the training college to become cadets for officership. While the young people's work had been limited during the time that the corps met under canvas, the opening of the new building stimulated an increase in attendance, and new corps cadets had been accepted as well. Specialised classes for boys and girls had been established.

Freewill cartridge giving by the soldiers completely paid for the officers' weekly allowances.[108]

Little wonder that Commissioner Hay promoted Staff-Captain Lonnie to the rank of Major and appointed him to be Divisional Secretary for the Brisbane Division in December 1912. As the *War Cry* report announcing this change indicated,

> Major Lonnie has behind him an excellent record of successful Field Work. At Sydney he has established a record in congregations, open-air attendance, soldier making, War Cry circulation and self-denial effort. During his command the old Temple has been replaced by the splendid Congress Hall, and by his personal effort portion of the required money was raised. He will go to Brisbane early in December, well qualified to support the Divisional Commander. We have no doubt that both the promotion and appointment will give general satisfaction.[109]

At their farewell, George was recognised as 'a man whose zeal was a principle, and not a feeling'. Jennie was recognised for her kind and gentle spirit who helped on the war. She was praised as 'a mother in the corps and loved by all, especially the young people, whom she worked amongst, and by whom she will be greatly missed'. A congregation of 730 attended their final public meeting.[110]

Ensign Mary Anderson, the frail and timid Captain who had joined the Lonnies as their assistant at Auckland in 1904, also farewelled, but this time to a separate appointment. She had developed wonderfully through working so closely with Jennie and George, revealing 'unexpected depths of resilience and character which persuaded Commissioner Hay to appoint her in 1913 to the Melbourne Police Court to assist women and girls in distress'.[111] Mary Anderson remained in that specialised sphere of work for the rest of her career. Although she officially retired in 1935, she carried on her work until 1946 when she was 71. She was the first woman officer in Australia to be admitted to the Order of the Founder in 1953 and was awarded the MBE in the Queen's Birthday Honours List of 1956 just prior to her promotion to Glory in August of that year. She remained a firm family friend of the Lonnies throughout her life. I recall 'the little Major', as she was affectionately called by those she helped in Melbourne, visiting my grandmother and mother during the time we lived in Thornbury, Victoria from 1950–55.

Brisbane Division, Queensland

For the next 13 months till January 1914, Major George Lonnie served as the Divisional Secretary for the Brisbane Division in Queensland.

This was a familiar area for George and Jennie as their first married appointment was at Brisbane 1 Corps in 1901, followed by service at Ipswich in 1902, and Toowoomba in 1903–04. Their daughters Ivy and Florrie settled into the young people's corps at West End.[112]

The Lonnies' official welcome into the division took place on a very warm Thursday, December 19. The welcome was as warm as the weather! The Divisional Commander, Brigadier E.A. Harris, spoke of his long association with Major Lonnie and his high esteem for his work together with his utmost satisfaction at his appointment as Divisional Secretary. In response Major Lonnie noted that, 'Through all the windings of life's pathway he traced the hand of God, and he had come to his new position to give the very best he was capable of to push on the Salvation War and win souls for His Master'.[113]

During the next few months George and Jennie visited many of the corps in the division and learned about the responsibilities of divisional leadership. Jennie documented some of their visits in articles in the pages of *The War Cry*. All this prepared them for their first responsibility as divisional leaders in the Newcastle division from January 1914 to January 1917.

CHAPTER 7

Divisional leadership

Newcastle Division 15 January 1914 to 4 January 1917

The experiences of almost 20 years in corps, social services and some divisional work provided an excellent preparation for George and Jennie as they took on the leadership of the Newcastle Division in 1914. Having inspired their soldiers in Australia, New Zealand and back in Australia, their task was now to inspire the officers in their division to provide similar leadership in the corps they commanded.

Anyone reading the reports of their visits to corps around the division could not help but be impressed by the energy with which they journeyed to centres, led meetings and preached from the Bible. Jennie provided enthusiastic leadership to the Home League and carried on her support for children's work throughout the division. George continued to be a dynamic preacher of salvation and holiness who would sometimes burst into song during a Bible message. Both of them led prayer meetings, open-air meetings, regular Sunday meetings and special meetings for Easter, always preaching for a verdict—never being satisfied unless souls responded to the messages. Jennie often spoke of her experiences in the social services work of The Salvation Army. Whilst always desiring to have enthusiastic workers in each corps, they never hesitated to farewell suitable candidates to go to the training college to be trained as officers.

The years they were in the Newcastle Division coincided with the First World War. A number of bandsmen volunteered or were called up for service, and their places needed to be taken by others. The National Anthem was sung at the end of meetings in senior citizens residences. Camp Institutes were set up at Newcastle, and Rutherford in West Maitland—the forerunners of Red Shield huts in the Second World War. At the opening of the Rutherford Centre in April 1916, George indicated that such Institutes were erected for the comfort and benefit of all soldiers. The facilities would provide for letter writing, reading and playing of clean games. Services would be conducted and entertainments provided from time to time as well.[114] George even advertised for a second-hand piano for the Rutherford Institute to assist with the entertainment and fellowship.[115]

The Monday night programme of the young people's anniversary at Newcastle Corps in late 1915 featured a platform with quite a 'military appearance—two tents, with the British flag waving, soldier boys, Red Cross nurses, stretchers and wounded etc.; whilst the bugle call was heard as the fireworks went off. Y.P.S.M. MacDonald looked very relieved at the close of the meeting.'[116] Ivy and Florrie were obviously active in that young people's corps and received full marks for their attendance, participation and learning during the year. Together with two other girls who similarly received full marks, they were delighted to receive some good books to read as their prizes.[117]

George and Jennie were sought-after specials for events such as harvest festivals. At most of these events, seekers were recorded. However, at East Maitland, the *War Cry* report sadly indicated that, 'The people gave of their cash, but refused to give themselves to God.'[118]

George officiated at the re-opening of Raymond Terrace Corps in 1915,[119] together with opening of new halls at East Maitland in early 1916[120] and at Kendall later the same year.[121] Kendall Corps, having been planted by Taree Corps originally, became the centre of a new district including Kew and Hannam Vale.[122] Jennie opened the new primary rooms for Glebeland Corps in April 1916.[123] Following an inspection tour by Staff-Captain Anderson, a number of corps halls were thoroughly renovated, including Glebeland, Lambton, Wallsend, Kurri Kurri, Singleton, Raymond Terrace, West Maitland and Newcastle.[124]

Lieutenant (later Captain) W.F. Harold Boase was appointed to assist the Lonnies and featured in many reports. George had known this officer who had been a young person when George was in charge of Adelaide City Corps 16 years earlier.[125] An accomplished musician, Captain Boase sometimes supported with cornet solos. Jennie's name increasingly became associated with the reports to *The War Cry* on progress in the division.[126] I suspect she also wrote under the pen names 'Faith' and 'Pioneer' from time to time.[127]

Industrial disputes around the Newcastle area in 1915–16, resulting in strikes spanning 41 weeks, caused the loss of £260,000 in wages alone. Despite such losses, Salvationists in Newcastle managed to increase their total giving from £250 to £300 that year. According to the relevant *War Cry* report, 'Major and Mrs Lonnie have toiled unceasingly to help to bring about the glorious results for which we now praise God. Our leaders conducted no fewer than 19 meetings in connection with the festivals; in fact, I heard the Major say he almost dreamt about straw, vegetables and fruit.'[128] In those 19 meetings, 21 sought salvation.[129]

With Kempsey becoming a corps in the Newcastle Division, George, Jennie and Captain Boase undertook a 12-day visit by a horse-drawn vehicle to the northern corps in the division in 1915. The tour took in Port Macquarie, Kempsey, Wauchope, Coopernook, Mitchells Island, Burrell Creek and Taree.[130]

As World War I continued, the ladies of the Home League, probably at the encouragement of Jennie, became increasingly involved in supporting the enlisted soldiers. For instance, it was reported that the West Maitland branch 'earned the respect and esteem of the boys in the Rutherford camp. Every alternate Thursday, a company of the league goes to the camp and repairs the boys' clothes, and darns their socks, etc., and a company from East Maitland take up the work the next week.'[131]

Toward the end of 1916, the Lonnies received news that they would be moving elsewhere. So they conducted tours around the division in November and December before more formal farewell gatherings early in January 1917. Many spoke words of appreciation to George and Jennie. Captain Boase spoke of the benefits and blessings received while serving with the Major in the office, and also 'the privilege of having being permitted to come under the influence of their home life'.

In response, Jennie thanked the officers, soldiers and friends for their kindness and help and expressed 'sincere regret having to leave Newcastle, and particularly the Home Leagues, which had come in for a large share of her time and labour'.[132] George rejoiced that during the past three years some 1,200 souls had sought salvation, the numbers of soldiers had increased, renovations to properties had been undertaken and new Army buildings erected. As result, all present were encouraged to lift their hearts in thankfulness to God for his goodness. As the meeting concluded, George, Jennie, Ivy and Florrie stood under the flag in dedication, whilst Captains Dennis and Grant sang 'I cannot leave the dear old flag'.[133]

East Melbourne Division 4 January 1917 to 17 March 1921

The offices of the divisional headquarters occupied rooms in the building of the Hawthorn Citadel at that time, so it was appropriate that George and Jennie were welcomed as leaders in a Sunday morning meeting in the Citadel led by the then Chief Secretary, Colonel Wiebe Palstra.

On being introduced by Colonel Palstra, Jennie's first remarks were, 'Because of my confidence in God, I know he'll never fail, and I am determined to do my best, to be or do just what he would have me.'

The War Cry report of the occasion indicated that before the applause died down after he was welcomed, George was leading in the singing of 'His Spirit I'm receiving'. After expressing appreciation for the hearty and extended welcome given to him and Jennie, George gave 'an earnest and eloquent address. A pointed and powerful appeal followed and a number of seekers came to the front in receiving the blessing of sanctification'.[134]

In the evening meeting both Jennie and George, unbeknown to each other, chose to speak on the text 'Repent ... and believe the gospel'. 'What we need is less preaching and more good living,' emphasised George.[135]

In a public installation meeting on the following night, Jennie spoke of the warmth of the welcome she had received, which dispelled any doubts that she might have been lonely amongst strangers. Her theme was 'Go Forward'. George emphasised that 'he had come to East Melbourne to preach Christ and him alone'. Nine seekers were recorded for salvation and sanctification that night, making a total of 20 over the course of the weekend.[136]

The emphases on preaching the gospel, endeavouring to bring the unsaved to Jesus and the sanctification of God's people, continued to be the themes of George and Jennie's preaching and teaching during the next four years in East Melbourne. They always preached for a decision—and many responded positively.

With her great love for young people's and women's work, Jennie encouraged development in both areas around the 50 corps, societies and outposts in the division.

As he had in the past, George encouraged corps and sections (such as brass bands) to become self-supporting, raising funds to ensure that the work could move forward. He was keen to boost *War Cry* sales and harvest festivals as good sources of income. As divisional commander, he was delighted to open new corps buildings and other similar facilities around the division. George encouraged uniform wearing by Salvationists and taking the gospel to 'unusual' places—for example, Brighton Beach—during public holidays such as Melbourne Cup Day and Australia Day. He was glad to recognise faithful service given by those receiving 'Never Absent Never Late' badges.

Ivy and Florrie sometimes shared in the activities of their parents. On one occasion when George and Jennie together with a divisional staff member were visiting Camberwell Girls Home, 27 of the girls stepped forward to make their decisions for Christ. The *War Cry* report of the event by Rose A. Griffiths noted: 'It did our hearts good to hear Florrie Lonnie pour out her heart to God on behalf of the kneeling penitents. Then one after another the girls lifted up voices to God in prayer, and our souls were stirred as we listened. Truly it was a wonderful time! God came near …'[137] Florrie was not quite 12 years of age at the time, but she was certainly being encouraged to pray in public and participate. She encouraged other young people, including me, to do the same thing decades later.

Toward the end of 1919 Florrie became seriously ill with pneumonia, probably triggered by the virus causing the current influenza epidemic. Many people prayed for her recovery. In praying for herself, Florrie promised to serve God as a Salvation Army officer. Seven years later, having fully recovered, she fulfilled that promise by entering training for officership in 1926.

George was promoted to the rank of Brigadier effective 2 August 1918, with Jennie taking the designation 'Mrs Brigadier Lonnie' in accordance with the tradition of the time.

Something of George's heart for the unsaved can be sensed by the following extract from a *War Cry* article he wrote to encourage participation in the 'The Great Call' Campaign of 1921.

'Watchman, how far is it into the night?'

These words are being continually asked of God's children, sometimes carelessly, sometimes contemptuously, merely inquisitively, but our hearts are cheered when we hear the question asked earnestly.

We, as his messengers on the watchtower, must be ever on the alert as to the answer we give. Isaiah, in his vision, saw the appalling darkness of the nation around him; so we must see the sin and indifference around us; yet, we must understand the world's night, the problems that perplex the minds of men, the tears, the burdens and sorrows, the strife and unrest, and we know the only remedy for all is the mind and spirit of Jesus; so let us be up and doing.

We thank God for the Army, for God's salvation, which has reached even to us. So let us ring out the message. Paul says, 'Woe is unto me if I would preach not the gospel.' The call comes to every one of us. What about our families, our neighbours, our work-mates, the business people we have to do with in our every-day life?

'Through God we shall do valiantly.' Let us win them for Christ during 1921.[138]

In support of the Campaign, half-nights of prayer were arranged and held at Canterbury, Hawthorn, Box Hill, Malvern, Brighton and Mordialloc, with more planned to follow. A report in *The War Cry* by 'Faith' a few months later noted that:

The Campaign is going well. Hard, barren places are being visited by God's power; backsliders are returning; souls are being saved; churchgoers attracted by the extra efforts, have sought God's power to save and bless; young women are consecrating themselves for officership. One feature of all these meetings has been that as different ones have left the mercy-seat, they have gone to deal with someone else. 'God forgive me for the bitter hatred I have had in my heart for 15 months,' was one audible prayer. Our officers have been cheered and blessed.[139]

In the midst of all these activities, George was appointed as the divisional leader to Western Australia, effective March 1921.

Western Australia Division 17 March 1921 to 22 October 1925

George was welcomed most heartily by Salvationists in Western Australia when he returned to become divisional commander. Having been a pioneer officer on the goldfields, welcomes commenced in Kalgoorlie and 'at intervals along the railway to Perth as many old-time Salvationists took the opportunity of congratulating their former pioneer field officer upon returning after 24 years to take over the command.'[140]

The welcomes continued on the family's arrival in Perth. A 'monster demonstration' consisting of an open-air meeting on the corner of Murray and Barrack Streets where 80 Salvationists were present commenced their installation event. In a large public meeting at Perth Fortress which followed, the new leaders were assured of the loyalty and support of officers and local officers of the division. 'Envoy Robert Palmer (Divisional Bandmaster) remarked that the Brigadier was the first pioneer officer of Western Australia to return to take charge of the Division. It was he who, as Captain Lonnie introduced him (the speaker) to the position of bandmaster; and dedicated his firstborn, Doris (who is now a cadet in training in Melbourne.) [In] representing the bands and local officers, the envoy assured the new commander and his family of their hearty cooperation.'[141]

In response, Jennie expressed appreciation for the cordiality of the welcome she had received. She testified to the way in which she had been led from 'an attitude of contempt for The Salvation Army to become one of its converts and [an] active and enthusiastic agent.'[142]

George called for ''Tis the old-time religion' and then opened his response to the welcome with reminiscences of his former experiences in the West, especially as skipper of the Perth Corps. He recalled that the services were conducted in a tent, at one time, on the spot near the present Fortress. He said he could never forget Perth for the kindness shown him by comrades and friends during his term as F.O. (field officer or corps officer) in that city. He also provided highlights into the hardships endured by the pioneer officers in Western Australia and took the opportunity of advising courage and determination in the present as well.[143] During the course of their Sunday meetings at Perth Fortress, there were 12 seekers for salvation and nine for holiness.

Because of George's earlier links with Perth Fortress, many thought that the family would soldier at that corps. Years later, I remember my mother telling me how her father asked the question,

'Which is the closest corps to our quarters?' On being told it was Highgate, George responded, 'My girls will attend Highgate.' He always encouraged soldiers to attend their nearest corps and his family would set the example. So the following Sunday, the Lonnies conducted meetings at Highgate with three comrades seeking the blessing of holiness and five seekers for salvation.[144]

Jennie was warmly welcomed by the ladies of the Home League throughout the state, and encouraged the opening of the leagues in many of the corps. Subsequent reports indicated that she stimulated a wide range of education and service events amongst the members. Very early on, in 1921, family members were encouraged to repair and alter garments for children who needed them because, even in sunny Western Australia, there was poverty and need.[145] In 1925, visiting speakers to Home League meetings were encouraged to speak about 'The Drink Evil'. Women leaguers helped to form part of a procession in the interests of Prohibition in the state that year.[146] In addition, Jennie gave lectures about the Army's work amongst deprived people in the slums of Australian cities, her experiences in New Zealand, and customs in China about which she must have researched or gleaned insights from furloughing missionaries.

George had only just taken command of the Western Australia Division when General Bramwell Booth paid a visit to Australia. With some background of the area and the people, together with good teamwork, the details of the General's reception and campaign were carried through very satisfactorily.

As usual, George and Jennie moved around all the corps in the division, from Geraldton to Albany and Perth to Kalgoorlie, preaching the message of salvation to the unsaved and encouraging holiness of life amongst soldiers. Many seekers were recorded. George and Jennie inspired officers, soldiers, corps cadets, junior soldiers and Sunday school members and their teachers. George was delighted to enrol many senior and junior soldiers.

After the Sunday morning meeting at Midland Junction, George had a pleasant surprise. A lady with three beautiful little children said she would like to speak to him and asked if he remembered her. When he said 'No,' she told the story of how some 27 years earlier he cared for her after her mother died and arranged for her to be adopted. When she described how he gave her water from his hands when she was thirsty on the journey to George's quarters from the camp where her father and brother lived, the memories came flooding back. How delighted he was to know that she was now happily married, with three lovely girls and was well saved! As he wrote in a report to *The War Cry* in 1925, 'So you can guess I was cheered to find that I had done a little bit of good work that had stood the test of time.'[147]

The effects of the Great War were still evident for many years after its conclusion in 1918. In a personal letter, George recalled how he had conducted the wedding of a former military soldier in 1921. This man had lost both his legs, yet George described him as 'a bright, happy young fellow'. The groom and his bride both came from Salvationist families. Two of the groom's attendants had each lost one leg and a third was completely blind as result of the ravages of the Great War.[148]

Always keen to improve the properties within his divisions, George announced that halls for the York and Guildford Corps had been purchased, funded as one of the last acts of Commissioner Hay as he left Australian shores.[149] A derelict hall at Menzies, an almost deserted mining town, was taken to pieces and moved 200 miles (320 kilometres) before being re-erected at Merredin, then a developing wheat-growing area. The block of land had been selected by George following inquiries with the Roads Boards office and personal inspection on a road trip around the area in a motor car owned by Adjutant Seaton.[150] George sought and was granted permission from the government to use the block for a hall. About a year later, he officially declared the building open to the glory of God and for the salvation of the people in Merredin and district.[151] In 1923 Perth Fortress citadel was enlarged and a primary room was added to the rear of the premises. By April 1924, four new corps had been opened, also five new senior halls, three new young people's halls, five new primary halls, three officers' quarters and two new band rooms.

In the 12 months from 1923 to 1924, numbers of new converts, soldiers and recruits in the division grew and total indoor attendances increased. So did the numbers attending open-air meetings, indoor Sunday and weekday meetings plus Home League and Y.P. attendances. Copies of *The War Cry* and *Young Soldier* sold increased by 21,185 and 10,254 respectively. Cartridge and other income increased as well.[152] On 14 April 1924, George was promoted to the rank of Lieut-Colonel, Jennie being designated as Mrs Lieut-Colonel.

George was always enthusiastic to improve the results of the Self Denial appeal. In 1922 £7,436 was raised in the division and a year later £7,443. Similarly, he encouraged generous Harvest Festival thanksgiving offerings. In 1925 he reported that 11 of the 15 corps comprising the division had exceeded their previous amounts by record margins and the four remaining reached their last year's figure.

The Christmas season each year was always full of activities. George and Jennie shared with social services officers and staff at Fremantle Prison ministry and made visits to various social service centres. Each year many Salvationists took the opportunity to enjoy a day's outing at Nedlands during the United Field Day, with open-air meetings held to proclaim the gospel on New Year's Day.[153]

During the Lonnies' term in Western Australia, Ivy and Florrie became increasingly active at the Highgate Corps. *War Cry* and *Young Soldier* reports indicate that they served as corps cadets. Ivy was commissioned as the Y.P. Sergeant-Major, life-saving guard leader, songster and member of the corps orchestra, in which she played the violin. During Congress meetings taking place when General Bramwell Booth visited Western Australia in 1924, she applied to become an officer. Ivy was accepted and commenced her formal officer training in March 1925. Florrie became the primary leader, life-saving guard chaplain, songster and a member of the corps orchestra, in which she played the mandolin.[154] In 1925 she served as the corps treasurer as well.

In 1924, Jennie's father, Brother Hammer of Ballarat, was promoted to Glory. His designation as 'brother' and the term 'promoted to Glory' suggest he may have become a Salvation Army soldier or was certainly an active Christian in another church, as was his wife.[155] Again, Jennie would not have been able to travel from her appointment in the West to attend his funeral.

As in other divisions, George encouraged public prayer. At Guildford, three half-nights of prayer were held in one month in connection with the 'Triumphant Tenth' Campaign in 1925. Many officers arranged for cottage meetings in outlying parts of their districts and extra weeknight meetings were well attended. Midday prayer meetings were held in Perth. During some of these occasions adults and young people sought salvation and holiness.[156]

With the pressures of most intense ministry, reports filtered through to THQ of a series of illnesses experienced by George and Jennie. Furloughs were not taken regularly in those days and seemed to be granted when an officer became so unwell that there was no other option but to give them opportunity to rest. In late 1925, George was given extended furlough of three months on account of his (unspecified) illness, before being appointed as the Candidates Secretary at Territorial Headquarters in Melbourne.[157]

Before George and Jennie departed from Perth, many took the opportunity to thank them for the leadership in the division over the past four years and seven months. 'The Colonel and his wife have laboured hard and have inspired officers of the field as well as officers of the men's and women's social work by their Christian lives.'[158]

The War Cry report of the farewell also contained a telling assessment by a good friend of the Army.

> Doctor Taylor Thomas, the Army's medical officer in West Australia, said that after knowing Colonel Lonnie about two years he had come to the conclusion that he is a disciplinarian. 'An organisation in which efficiency counts must not have a putty man at the head of affairs.' He had seen the Army at work in Paris, South Africa and other places, and looked upon it with profound admiration. 'To do the grand work that the Army is doing you must have

level-headed men and women at the head. Colonel Lonnie
has always impressed me by being such.'[159]

In thanking those present at their farewell for their good wishes
George outlined some of the advances made in Western Australia
during the period of their leadership.

> Three new corps had been opened; three YP and seven
> primary halls are being erected. Eleven senior halls were
> renovated as well as six YP halls. Fifty-three cadets had
> entered the Training Garrison, and 11 accepted candidates
> were waiting to enter the Garrison next session. Over
> £37,000 [$74,000] had been raised for Self-Denial and the
> Harvest Festival appeal had just doubled.[160]

George went on to thank the DHQ staff and men's and women's social
officers as well as the corps officers, local officers and soldiers for all
the help they had been during his term in Western Australia.

A united Home League farewell was afforded to Jennie. Each of
the speakers referred to her hard work in connection with the Home
League movement in Western Australia during those years.

So the divisional leadership phase of their faithful service
concluded, and fresh opportunities would open up for them back in
Victoria.

CHAPTER 8

Territory-wide opportunities

The arrival of the Lonnies back in Melbourne for extended furlough meant they were present for the commissioning of the Eureka Session which had been trained at the Training Garrison in 1925.[161] Ivy was commissioned and given the rank of Cadet-Sergeant for the following year. A fellow cadet-sergeant from the same session was Allen Sharp. He was an officers' son, who had been a compositor at the Army's Printing Works, an accomplished cornet player and had been deputy bandmaster at the Melbourne City Temple Corps before entering College.

The Lonnies' accommodation was at 57 Woolton Avenue, Thornbury. This location provided an opportunity for Florrie, who had also felt God's call to officership on her life, to make her application to the next training session. As a result, she was farewelled to the College from the Thornbury Corps rather than from the Highgate Corps in Western Australia. She joined five other candidates from the Thornbury Corps, including Margaret (Madge) Arnott, William (Bill) Jewell, Alice Roach (who eventually married Bill Jewell) and Eric Wilkinson. In the few months before entering the Garrison, Florrie served as Intermediate-Leader in the Y.P. Corps.[162]

The Lonnie family, c. 1927, from left:
Florence, George, Ivy and Jennie.

Candidates Secretary 12 April 1926 to 10 April 1928

After about five months furlough, George was well enough to resume work and was appointed by the General as the Candidates Secretary for the territory. Having successfully recruited candidates for officership from the corps and divisions he commanded over the years, he now had the opportunity of encouraging corps and divisional officers to do the same. He also had a particularly sympathetic understanding of candidates because his two daughters had recently entered the Training Garrison.[163]

George and Jennie took every opportunity of conducting meetings and preaching at corps around the Melbourne area and beyond, resulting in regularly seeing seekers at the mercy-seat. By the end of the year, 67 candidates were accepted for the 1927 training session.

Perhaps on a recommendation by George, the Territorial Commander, Commissioner Hugh E. Whatmore, issued a directive that a Candidates Sunday would be held on 18 July 1926, 'when special effort must be made to secure strong, consecrated young men and women as candidates for Salvation Army officership'.[164] In support of this special Sunday, George had an extensive interview with the editor of *The War Cry* which was published under the title 'Heeding God's Call'.[165] He commenced by rightly indicating that 'the salvation of the unconverted is the highest purpose to which any person can devote his or her life.' He continued, 'There may be much disagreement concerning the choosing of the next most important vocation, but there can be no doubt that direct full-time service for God is the highest employment open to men and women; and for Salvationists, officership is the medium of that service.' George went on to point out that this calling is not necessarily open to all. 'For there are limitations of character, of health and probability that have a direct bearing on the question of officership but presuming that my words are addressed to converted persons, I would say that the decision of these questions may be safely left to the officers appointed by headquarters to consider the acceptance of candidates.' He continued,

> More important to the young Salvationist is a question of Divine selection. God calls! I am fully persuaded, both by my own personal experience and by the observations of a life spent in Salvation Army service, that God definitely calls to officership those whom he desires to serve in that way. The question all young Salvationists must face is 'Does God call me?'

> There are many blessings that follow a glad hearkening to the voice of God, and ready obedience to his call. To three of these only would I refer just now.[166]

In outlining the blessing of peace, George related how he lost his own peace as a young man by resisting God's call to officership as outlined in the first chapter of this book (pages 4 and 5).

'The second reward of obedience is power. Those whom God calls for service he also makes fit. God never makes a fool of any man, though he does sometimes test him,' continued George.

> Just as he called upon Abraham to offer his son Isaac as a sacrifice, and then, when Abraham proved his willingness, allowed him to retain his son, so God today sometimes calls to officership men and women who are physically unfit,

and then, when they honour him by placing themselves upon his altar and applying for officership, he says, 'No, I have proved your faith; it is enough. Serve where you are.' For such he has a special reward of grace such as he had for beloved Abraham. It is not the prerogative of the person called to say to God 'I am unfit.' For God most wonderfully empowers those whom he needs.[167]

George went on to describe the effects of obedience on a young woman in the East Melbourne Division when he was the divisional commander there. She came from a background in which she had been abused by her parents and become resistant to many expressions of love. When she applied to become an officer, George was dubious about the matter. 'She had certainly improved wonderfully since her conversion; but was she fit for the great work of officership? God guides in these matters, however, and the girl was accepted.' He went on to describe how she had performed remarkably well in a corps appointment which had previously been very difficult, but now under her direction was thriving. When she found the present corps hall was too small, she raised the money needed to renovate and expand the hall. 'You see,' he continued, 'God had called her. He had also empowered her for service.'

Having touched on peace and power, George went on to point out that the third result of obedience is joy. 'No joy on earth can compare with that which comes from successful soul-winning.' He then described how the Army had sent a young man to an important mining centre some years before. Other divisional staff feared that the task would be too heavy for the lad but George believed the appointment to be God's will. He described how radiantly happy the young man was when several notorious drunkards got soundly converted in his meetings.

So enthused was he that he would be up before the sun to hurry to the home of the latest convert, there to sit and read to him and as he had his breakfast, offer a word of prayer, walk with him to the pit's mouth and then leave him with a warm handclasp and a prayer for God's blessing. The joy of it all was beyond belief! Work? Yes, any amount. Responsibility? Yes, enough to crush many another young fellow. Cares? Yes, in abundance. But through all and above all a joy that nothing on earth could quench.

Yes, peace, and power, and joy unbounded are the lot of those who gladly obey the call of God.[168]

George continued by talking about those who turn away from the call; the disappointment, sorrow, distress and the grim tragedy which marks their every step in the future. His own experience and that of many others reflected lost peace, bitter condemnation and continual discontent. While some were able to take the opportunity to make amends, for others circumstances arose that made their later acceptance impossible.[169]

George made an excellent Candidates Secretary and stirred many to make their own application for officership. He had a target for 115 acceptances for the next training session, a figure considerably greater than the results achieved during the previous year. By the end of December 1926, 90 cases had been finalised and a number of other cases were under consideration with the hope of being finalised by the end of February 1927.[170] In the event, 95 candidates were finally accepted to enter training in March, of which 50 had been corps cadets and seven were officers' children.[171] Amongst those seven officers' children were the brothers William Bramwell Southwell and David John Southwell of Kew Corps in Victoria.

Never a person to wait for people to come to him, George always moved out to meet people. Together with Major Percy Dean from the Training College staff he made a successful tour of the Adelaide and Peterborough Divisions in South Australia early in 1927.[172] The purpose was to recruit more candidates for officership and conduct evangelical meetings. Major Dean had served in India and was able to speak of the missionary work of The Salvation Army in that land, whereas George could speak about his pioneering activities in Australia.[173]

Jennie's enthusiasm for and experience in women's work was recognised in the middle of 1927 when she was appointed as the Territorial Home League Secretary. She succeeded Mrs Colonel Gaskin. In responding to words of welcome from the various corps Home League secretaries in the Melbourne Division at Carlton Corps (where, incidentally, her daughter Captain Ivy Lonnie was then the corps officer), Jennie said that at first she had shrunk from the idea of taking on the position but 'after prayer had accepted it at the hands of God. In his strength she was determined to do all in her power to help womankind.'[174]

She was formally welcomed into the position by Mrs Commissioner Whatmore on 18 August 1927 at the Brunswick Citadel. Mrs Whatmore emphasised that Jennie's 29 years of officership 'gave her a wide and practical experience of womanhood and motherhood.' Mrs Colonel Orames pointed out that, 'Mrs Colonel Lonnie commended herself to women of the Army because amongst other things, she had so trained her own children that they had become workers for God.' In response, Jennie said, 'All I have shall be placed at the disposal of every league and every leaguer. I am yours for service.'[175]

Jennie was also warmly welcomed into the position by the Home Leaguers of Ballarat. On that occasion Jennie reminisced about the night 31 years previously when she made her decision to follow Christ and promised that she would devote her life to the saving of girls and women. She realised that this new appointment provided a special opportunity for this service and was determined to make the most of it.[176]

At a similar welcome meeting in Geelong, Jennie urged the members to aim at continued progress. To do otherwise would mean stagnation to the cause. 'We must introduce new people, and increase our numbers,' she said, 'and this responsibility rests with every Home League member.'[177]

In the meantime, George continued to encourage the recruitment of candidates. In a conversation with the editor of *The War Cry* for the Candidates' Sunday edition in August 1927, George emphasised the great and growing need for officers because 'our borders will always extend at a greater rate than we can possibly recruit workers'.[178] These should be the very best in every corps—and even from outside the Army provided they are godly and love souls. He pointed out that the Regulations indicated that 'the Candidate ought to possess some energy and character, and a spirit of determination to succeed.'[179]

He also sought to clarify many points of potential misunderstanding. For instance, George pointed out that … 'It is idle to suppose that people without brains are either wanted as officers or even supposing they were allowed to become officers that they would get anywhere in the Army. The nature of the work demands constant mental alertness and vigour. Whatever brains a person may fortunately be endowed with that person will not be of much use in the Army unless accompanying the brains is a passion for the souls of the people and an absolute abandonment to God.'[180]

He also pointed out that many of the brightest and best candidates for officership came from small corps rather than large ones. Whilst corps officers of such small corps might be resistant to giving up their best soldiers for officership when the fighting forces are small, God honours such a sacrifice. He used an example of a small corps in one of the divisions he commanded. The corps officer there was greatly concerned when two of his best soldiers became candidates. Their going meant that half the band and a third of the open-air fighters as well as the best of the young people's workers in the corps were departing. 'God so honoured the sacrifice made by the corps that a spiritual awakening occurred, and within three months of the candidates leaving, the corps marched over 30 strong,' George said.[181]

When asked about the most significant sources of supply of candidates, George quickly pointed out that corps cadets provided the largest number of candidates at that time. Of the 27 candidates already accepted for the next session, all 27 had been corps cadets. While the age limits for candidates were normally between 18 and 25 years of age at that time, some flexibility was possible. He spoke of the man who was well above the age limit who was not a Salvationist when he first made application, but was well saved and desired earnestly to give up his life for service in the Army. He had his own farm with good prospects ahead of him, but was willing to sacrifice all this for the sake of the Kingdom. He travelled over 370 miles (590 kilometres) to see the corps officer and the divisional commander and to attend weekend meetings of the Army. Since then he has become a recruit, signed the Articles of War and was now waiting to take the next step into officership. George added, 'You will agree that it would be a thousand pities to debar that man from realising his ambitions merely because he is a little over the stipulated age.' In that context, I was interested to recall that George was 26 when he became a cadet.

Accompanying the article was a photograph of the Candidates Secretary in a strikingly similar pose to that of Lord Kitchener, then British Secretary of State for War in 1914, when he was advertising for soldiers for World War 1. While the caption of that Alfred Leete advertisement read: 'Your country wants you', in George's case, the caption read, 'Will you decide for officership today?'[182]

Will you decide for officership today?

By the end of October 1927, George reported to *The War Cry* that 53 candidates had been accepted for the 1928 training session and that there were a further 114 applications to be dealt with.[183] In the event, 63 candidates eventually entered the Training College as cadets in March 1928.[184]

Having successfully recruited some 153 candidates during the last two years, George was appointed as the Secretary for Special Efforts from 11 April 1928. As a divisional commander, George had a reputation for being an excellent organiser. The *War Cry* report announcing his new position noted that when he had taken up the command of the Perth Division, General Bramwell Booth was due to visit Australia soon afterwards. George had carried through all the arrangements for the General's reception and campaign down to the finest detail. In his new role he would …

> take over the organisation of the Congress Campaign which includes a great deal of worrying detail and will do so without being either flustered or forgetful. The Colonel, who has a wide experience of the Field, sound judgement, a right sense of discipline, a warm heart, and a deep knowledge of God, will be a valuable support to the Commissioner, and will command the ready support of the divisional commanders and others whose responsibilities for making and carrying out arrangements will be interwoven with his own.[185]

Jennie continued in her appointment as Territorial Home League Secretary. She had recently won the second prize for overseas competitors in a competition run by *The Officer* magazine (a magazine for officers published by International Headquarters in London) on the topic 'How successfully to run the home league'.[186]

Her enthusiasm for women's work knew no bounds. Wherever she could she encouraged members not simply to settle down because attendances were satisfactory and the meetings enjoyable, 'but to seek out women who were in need and invite them to the meetings.'[187] As she travelled around the territory, Jennie held her audiences spellbound as she related some of her experiences as a pioneer officer of slum work in Adelaide—especially how girls were rescued from lives of sin.[188] As 1928 commenced, she wrote in an article for *The War Cry*:

> The Home League must march forward. I want a recruiting campaign to be carried on in every corps by women who will pledge themselves to bring, if only, one new member to the League during the first half-year.
>
> All around us are women who need help. Invite them, visit them, call and bring them with you. Very many women have been helped and blessed through the league, so let us pass on the blessing to others.
>
> A hearty welcome to membership of the league awaits any girl or woman over the age of 18. We shall be especially glad to see the young mother with her baby. The mother who, because of the children, cannot attend a night meeting [of the corps], the Home League is for you. Join the Thrift Club; it will make you and yours happier. Branches of the league are re-opening the second week in February, which will be a good opportunity to join.
>
> To the members I would say, do all you can to make folk happy. Never let a day pass without doing someone a good turn. I am depending on everyone, and not merely the locals [local officers], to secure new members.[189]

She viewed the task of the Home League as making useful women and happy homes—especially during those years of economic depression.[190]

George and Jennie were delighted when their eldest daughter, Captain Ivy Lonnie, married Captain Allen Sharp on 22 November 1928. Ivy and Allen had come to know each other as cadets in 1925 and then the following year as cadet-sergeants at the Training College. Ivy served as the corps officer at Carlton Corps in 1928. Allen assisted in what was then called 'propaganda work' in 1927 and became the corps officer at Port Melbourne in 1928.

George and Jennie continued to conduct stirring evangelical meetings around the territory at corps, social services and in prisons.

Their emphasis was always on the salvation of the unsaved and the sanctification of God's people. Numerous seekers were recorded.

At a united Home League gathering in 1928, Jennie reported on the progress of the league's operations. She mentioned one league which, though only in operation for two years, had provided 900 garments and two prams for needy people; also two double beds and blankets, aside from other needed articles. At another league a sewing class for mothers was in operation under the supervision of an efficient instructor. During the year the Bendigo Division had opened two new leagues, Ballarat had opened one, Melbourne East three and Tasmania five.[191]

Jennie was always pleased to share stories of the effective ministry of the Home League in those days.

> Hearing of the death of a child, a Home League visitor called at the home of the stricken parents, and she found them to be in poor circumstances; so the funeral expenses were met by the Home League. Impressed by this practical form of religion the parents came to the meetings, became converted and later were enrolled as soldiers. The mother is now a Home League enthusiast and the children attend the young people's meetings.
>
> Another interesting story comes from the Ballarat division... During visitation a home leaguer found a family in dire need. At once the league supplied them with food and firing [a means of cooking the food]. Seeing the family occupied a house which they found even in normal times to be beyond their means, the league helped them to obtain a cheaper dwelling. Employment was found for her husband in a business house in the town. Since then the man has been transferred to a branch of the business in another district, and the wife has linked up with a Home League in that centre.[192]

She concluded her report by saying that a family campaign had been started, its objective being a 25 percent increase in weekly attendances, membership, Thrift Club membership, and local officers, especially visiting sergeants.[193] Jennie certainly believed in setting simple, measurable, achievable, resourced and time-based goals.

With 1929 being the centenary of the birth of the Army's Founder, William Booth, Jennie was pleased to announce that the Commissioner had kindly arranged that part of the Founder's Centenary Campaign in the month of October would be devoted to the interests of the Home League, a branch of which the Commissioner was anxious to see established at every corps throughout the Australia Southern Territory. She went on to write:

> The family is truly a most important branch of Salvation Army work. Any agency that is calculated to raise the standards of home life in the community, to benefit women generally and to help girls, is of the utmost value, not only to the Army but to the nation and indeed the whole world.
>
> The principal thought in the heart of Mrs General [Bramwell] Booth, our World President, in forming the Home League, was the gathering in and helping and blessing of women who, on account of home ties were unable to attend ordinary Salvation Army meetings, women whose circumstances were against them; women who had not made good wives and mothers.[194]

In order to help these women, successful housewives and good women were enlisted as league secretaries. She then indicated that during the last 21 years that the league had existed, a wonderful work been done in teaching women the right way to keep the house clean, to prepare nourishing meals, to practise thrift and to make clothing for their children. As result 'incompetent women have become wise and useful in consequence of the instruction and encouragement given'.[195]

Jennie challenged each woman Salvationist to become involved in the work of the Home League. Corps officers were encouraged to open new leagues and secure new members. 'Specials' were to be enlisted to conduct occasional meetings and bring blessing to the girls and women who attend the league. And Jennie concluded, 'Our motto is "Forward!"'[196]

At the Congress Home League Assembly in 1929, presided over by Mrs Commissioner Whatmore, Jennie had the opportunity of reporting on the work of the league to the end of 1928. According to *The War Cry* report, the most interesting statistics were: increase in membership, 1,198; increase in attendance, 492; increase in Thrift Club membership 156; increase in Home League local officers, 105. A total of £6,458 had been banked in the Thrift Club by the Home League members during 1928. Through the monthly spiritual meetings, eight women in one league alone were converted and enrolled as Salvation Army soldiers. At another league, 650 garments, 25 pair of boots, 429 loaves of bread, 424 baskets of food and a number of blankets and parcels of small goods were given away. At this league 15 babies were dedicated to God and the Army. At another league, 450 loaves of bread, 50 dozen buns, 160 tins of biscuits and 500 parcels of clothing were distributed. Mrs Commissioner Whatmore introduced Jennie with these words: 'I cannot speak too highly of her splendid work.'[197]

Although not included in his official career card, George acted as the divisional leader for the Melbourne Division for some five months early in 1929 before the welcome of Lieut-Colonel and Mrs McClure.[198] George was pleased to report that during the first four months of the year, 615 persons sought salvation in the division, and 200 claimed the blessing of holiness. In the same period 87 senior and 62 junior soldiers were enrolled. Property advances during that period included the erection of primary halls at Fairfield and Sunshine and the provision of officers' and band rooms at the same two corps.[199]

The final months of 1929 however, were clouded by the consequences of a serious accident to their daughter Ivy, now Mrs Captain Allen Sharp. While being driven to the Brighton Hospital to visit a sick young person from the Sunshine Corps, owing to the slippery condition of the road in late June, the car skidded and crashed head-on into a tree. The impact was so great that Ivy, who was sitting in the back seat, was thrown upward in the car and struck her head against the bar supporting the (soft) hood, fracturing the base of her skull. No seat belts were installed or required in those days. Ivy was admitted to the Alfred Hospital and was unconscious for more than a week. Obviously, her husband Captain Allen, her sister Captain Florrie, as well as George and Jennie were greatly distressed about this, but witnessed to being 'wonderfully upheld by the prayers and sympathy of their comrades'. It was a full five weeks before Ivy could leave the hospital and continue her recuperation at George and Jennie's home in Thornbury, and a total of 16 weeks after the accident before she was well enough to attend a meeting at the Sunshine Corps again. Continuing in a corps appointment would be impossible for some time, so Allen was reassigned from Sunshine Corps to work in the Finance Department at Territorial Headquarters in October.[200] By 1932, Ivy was well enough to share with Allen in corps appointments at Camberwell, South Fitzroy and Malvern through until 1937.[201]

Obviously, Ivy's need of support meant that Jennie could not travel too far out of Melbourne during most of 1930. She was an effective Home League special at suburban corps such as South Richmond, Northcote East, Fairfield, Coburg and Mordialloc. She did travel as far as Broadford on one occasion.[202] Ivy and Allen were eventually able to accompany George and Jennie in support of the Chief Secretary, Colonel W.A. Suttor, in November 1930 during a visit to Wonthaggi Corps and participated with speaking and singing.[203]

Some of Jennie's talks as a visiting special were most memorable. In one of her addresses on 'Light', members present were led to examine their hearts before God when she likened the powerful x-ray to the light of God piercing the inmost recesses of the heart.'[204] In another she used the letters H-O-M-E as the basis of an acrostic emphasising the importance of Harmony, Organisation, Methods and Economy for happiness in the family.[205]

At this time, Captain Florrie Lonnie successfully passed her final examination at Bethesda Hospital to qualify as a general and midwifery nurse. Rather than moving on to infant welfare studies, she undertook a special six months course in dietetics at the Melbourne Hospital.[206]

By July 1931, Jennie was able to report that 'in every division, leagues are being brought into existence and old ones revived'. A new Home League had commenced at Pinnaroo in South Australia. The league at Maryborough had been reorganised after a lapse of five or six years, with 14 members gained and 10 of these involved in the thrift club. New leagues had been opened at Mitcham and also Yallourn Corps. She noted that, '37 leagues are now operating in the Melbourne Central Division, every one showing signs of progress'.[207] Jennie recognised the good leadership given by the divisional home league secretaries in each of the divisions.[208]

CHAPTER 9

Retirement

Having completed 'thirty-eight years of courageous warfare against sin, and in the service of the needy', Lieut-Colonel George Lonnie entered honourable retirement on 31 October 1931 at the age of 65.[209] A public farewell took place on 10 November. In the official announcement it was noted that Jennie would continue her Home League duties until the end of the year—and more particularly until after the visit to the territory of General and Mrs Higgins. Jennie was not quite 62, in good health and had proved to be an exceedingly effective Territorial Home League Secretary.

As he approached retirement, George told, through the pages of *The War Cry,* the story of the motherless child for whom he secured a good foster home during his time at Guildford in Western Australia in 1895.[210]

The story of his pioneering exploits in Western Australia, and a summary of his activities in New Zealand and Australia became a *War Cry* feature article entitled, 'Well Fought, Comrades'.[211]

The last sixth of the lengthy article was headed, 'The Colonel's Better Half'. Jennie had been an officer for 32 years and when she became one she had no thought of any other sphere of Army service than being a social officer. 'I felt called to that work,' she said, 'and though I spent only two and a half years in social institutions and slum work, I have endeavoured in all my appointments to do social service.' The final three paragraphs of this article are worth quoting in full:

Since August 1927, Mrs Lonnie has been the Territorial Home League Secretary, which position she will not relinquish until the end of the present year.

During her term of office, the Home League has made outstanding progress and its self-sacrificing members have rendered noble work to the nation in its time of depression and need. Mrs Lonnie has been a moving spirit in this effort to help the unfortunate, and her example has been a constant source of inspiration to all who served under her.

It is a very great joy to the Colonel and his wife to know that, while they are compelled to step aside from front-rank fighting, their two daughters remain in the thick of the salvation fight. Captain Florrie is a valued member of 'Bethesda' Hospital staff. The other daughter (Ivy) is Mrs Captain Sharp of THQ.

An article was published in her hometown newspaper, *Ballarat Courier,* reporting on Jennie's retirement and that she was a niece of Mr J.J. Brokenshire of Ballarat. It related how Mrs Commissioner McKenzie, the wife of the Territorial Commander, commended Jennie for the wonderful work and progress of the Home League over the last five years, 'which was largely due to the work which Mrs Lonnie had put in... The wonderful Christian spirit abroad in the league was, to a great extent, due to the inspiration of Mrs Lonnie.'

In her response, Jennie told of her fearfulness when taking up the task of being the Territorial Secretary, but that she had always 'striven to do her best, and that God had blessed.' The report continued:

The League had certainly progressed, and that, she felt, was due to the practical work done by the individual leagues. To the divisional secretary, the local secretaries, the specials and every local officer, Mrs Lonnie offered thanks for the splendid service they had rendered.

> Mrs Lonnie was presented with a handsome auto-tray complete with drawers and cupboards, and bearing a suitable engraved shield. Other gifts were a rose bowl, full of carnations and a hand-painted carved wood vase, as personal testimonies to her popularity.
>
> Mrs Lonnie, whose parents resided many years in this district, received all her early 'Army' training in Ballarat, and her first Sunday school teacher still is associated with the work here and naturally very proud of her brilliant pupil.[212]

Following Ivy's steady recovery after that serious motor vehicle accident, George and Jennie's first grandchild, Isabel Sharp, was born in 1933. There was great rejoicing at Isabel's safe arrival.

George and Jennie were also delighted when their younger daughter, Captain Florrie, fell in love with Captain David John Southwell. David was the son of faithful officers, the late Field-Major David and Mrs Field-Major Sarah Southwell. At that time David was serving at the Finance Department at Territorial Headquarters and was a member of the Melbourne Staff Band. As mentioned earlier, Florrie had completed specialist diet studies. Consequently, she was in charge of food preparation at the Army's Bethesda Hospital when David became a patient there. He had almost lost his life due to peritonitis following a ruptured appendix and he needed specialised food to assist his recovery. In the process of his recovery, they commenced to pay attention to each other and friendship developed. Florrie and David married in Salvation Army uniform on 29 December 1934 at the Melbourne City Temple in a ceremony conducted by Colonel Ambrose Henry, the Financial Secretary. Ivy was the matron of honour.

An extensive report appeared in the newspaper *The Argus* two days later outlining the solemnity of the 'soldiers' wedding', held under 'the banner of the Army, signifying the Blood of sacrifice, the baptism of the Holy Spirit, and the purity of life' to which they were called.[213] The Melbourne Staff Band provided the accompaniment to the congregational singing as well as a 'sacred song'. 'After the ceremony the bride's small niece, Isabel Sharp, was led on to the dais and she presented the bride with a lovely bouquet of Madonna lilies and fragrant trails of sweet peas.'

The report concluded that, 'After the service the bride's parents entertained relatives of both families at their home in Thornbury.'[214]

Wedding reception for David and Florrie at the Lonnies'
home, 29 December 1934, with David's mother, Mrs
Field-Major Sarah Southwell, at left and Florrie's
mother, Mrs Lieut-Colonel Jennie Lonnie, at right.

Because of a lack of Salvation Army accommodation during those depression years, George and Jennie opened their home in Woolton Avenue, Thornbury, to Florrie and David until 1942. They shared their daughter's delight when she conceived and then the devastation when the full-term baby, who the parents named John, was stillborn—strangled by the umbilical cord in a slow labour.

On turning 70 in November 1936, a brief article outlining George's life was published in *The War Cry*. It concluded with a birthday message from Lieut-Colonel Lonnie which read as follows:

I would urge young officers of the present day to watch for the first appearance of evil, to protect their people from worldliness, to keep up the standard of holiness with a strong faith in a conquering Saviour. I have had no regrets for having made an unconditional surrender to God.

"Wherefore come out from among them, and be separate, saith the Lord, and touch not the unclean thing; and I will receive you. And will be a Father unto you, and ye shall be my sons and daughters, saith the Lord Almighty"[215] (2 Corinthians 6:17–18 KJV).

No doubt the Lonnies experienced the usual the rollercoaster of emotions common to other service personnel's parents when David was appointed as a Salvation Army chaplain to the Australian Imperial Forces soon after the commencement of World War II. What would the future hold for him, for their daughter, and for Australia?

However, David never spent any more than three months as an active military chaplain. He was appointed to Darnley Training Camp where he contracted scarlet fever, followed by an attack of Bell's Palsy. His condition was so serious that he needed 12 months sick leave in order to recover. During that time, I was conceived. When David had improved sufficiently, he was appointed to the office of The Salvation Army Chief Secretary to compile records of the Army's military work. I was born on 19 June 1942 at Bethesda Hospital and given the full name David Ian Southwell. To save confusion with my father I was always called Ian.

Soon after I was born, Florrie and David were appointed to Western Australia, David to become the Divisional Young People's Secretary effective September 1942. Although George and Jennie together with Florrie and David were officer-soldiers at the Thornbury Corps, I gather I was dedicated at the Lonnies' home. George's health was becoming increasingly fragile. After so many years of being part of their very close family, George and Jennie would have felt the significant loss of my parents and their newest grandchild moving to the other side of the continent. Ivy, Allen and Isabel were still in

Adelaide where Allen had been appointed as the Divisional Young People's Secretary for South Australia in 1940. The Sharps returned to Melbourne in October 1942 when Allen was appointed as the sub-manager of the Printing Works, and a year later became the manager.

George had been diagnosed with a heart condition and so it was not surprising that eventually on Friday afternoon, 18 June 1943, sitting quietly at the family fireside and just before Jennie bought him afternoon tea that, as *The War Cry* report noted, George's 'brave spirit had gone venturing into the Realms Beyond.'[216] The funeral service was conducted at the Thornbury Hall the following day by Commissioner Robert Henry (R). Major Allen Sharp brought a tribute in which he spoke of his father-in-law's well-balanced life. Messages were also telegraphed from my parents in Perth and General George Carpenter in London. The message from General Carpenter read as follows: 'It is with gratitude that I acknowledge Lieut-Colonel Lonnie's fifty years of whole-souled Salvationism and aggressive warfare for God and souls. God grant that, through his example, many of like spirit may rally to the Banner of the Cross in these eventful days.'

Before the committal at Fawkner Crematorium, Major Herbert Sheldrick spoke of the Colonel's example as a divisional commander, his thoroughness in inspections and his faithfulness and love in dealing with cases of difficulty.

The eulogy statement on the back of the order of service for his funeral was headed 'Four-Square Champion'. The first paragraph read:

> Within a week or two of fifty years ago, George W. Lonnie left his corps at Brunswick, when he was almost 27 years of age, to become a Salvation Army officer, and during the half-century which ensued, he won a worthy reputation for four-square championship of righteousness and truth, with uncompromising fearlessness in conflict against evil for the salvation of humanity. This warfare he waged in each of the mainland States of the Commonwealth of Australia and in New Zealand.[217]

Although I cannot remember it, my mother took me with her and flew across to Melbourne in the weeks following her father's funeral. With the help of her sister Ivy and brother-in-law Allen, she arranged to bring her mother back to Perth to live with us. Ivy and Allen were not in a position to look after Jennie because they were now caring for Allen's parents, Commandant and Mrs Sharp, and sharing a house with them in Swallow Street, Preston.

Thus commenced the 11 precious years, mentioned in the Preface of this book, in which I valued the interactions with my grandmother Jennie as well as my own parents. Grandma Lonnie moved with us from Perth to Melbourne when my father was appointed as the Divisional Young People's Secretary in 1945. Ten months later, in January 1946, my parents were appointed to the Western Victoria Division with headquarters in Ballarat as divisional leaders. Returning to Ballarat was a special delight for Jennie as it was almost a homecoming. The location provided an opportunity for her to have contact with her brother George Hoskin Hammer ('Hock', for short), who was still alive—although he was badly injured in a motor vehicle accident just near our house in Errard Street while coming to visit Jennie on one occasion.

Jennie was a great encourager and story teller. She loved to recite poetry and encouraged me to do so as well. One of her most memorable recitations was about the Inchcape Rock. The morality tale in poetic form related how a pirate captain of a ship cut the rope holding a warning bell to a buoy near the notorious Inchcape Rock. Years later his own ship foundered on the same rock one stormy night because the warning bell had gone and he drowned. The message was clear: sin has consequences—sometimes directly against the perpetrator.

Jennie was delighted when I made my decision to ask Jesus to be my Saviour. When my parents both had to be away attending meetings with officers and on other events that I could not attend, she readily looked after me. She joined in Bible readings from *The Soldier's Guide* after each meal and shared in our prayer-times. Over the years, her health, eyesight and mobility decreased. These disabilities became increasingly so after my parents were appointed to Melbourne Metropolitan Division in late 1950. She totally lost her sight.

For events such as officers' fellowships when they needed to be away, my parents asked one of their older peers, Mrs Colonel Anna Suttor, for support. Jennie knew Anna. She also hailed from Ballarat and was a relative of CSM Monod who had dealt with Jennie at the time she was making her own decision for Christ as mentioned in Chapter 4. Other visitors to Jennie included Major Mary Anderson, who also lived in Melbourne, as well as Captain Gladys Callis and other missionaries for whom Jennie was praying or with whom our family had contact.

Jennie grieved deeply when her granddaughter, Isabel Sharp, contracted poliomyelitis in throat and chest in 1953. Salk vaccine had not yet become available to prevent this deadly disease. Ivy and Allen were the divisional leaders in South Australia and they travelled urgently to Melbourne when Isabel took ill. They stayed at our home for the relatively short time Isabel was in Fairfield Infectious Diseases Hospital. Isabel's life ended within a fortnight of diagnosis, despite many fervent prayers and the best that medical science could do at that time—such as placing her in an iron lung to assist her breathing. Isabel was only 19, a lovely Salvationist and an excellent pianist.

Jennie Lonnie and the author as a boy on
possibly her 83rd birthday in 1953.

Despite such griefs and personal disabilities, Jennie retained her strong faith in her Saviour Jesus Christ. Eventually on the evening of Tuesday 4 May 1954, it was Jennie's time to go home to God. My parents were with her. I recall my mother telling me that just as the Lord's call came, Grandma opened her eyes wide and seemed clearly to see the glories beyond. To my mother it seemed to be a fulfilment of God's promise to Zechariah, 'At evening time it shall be light' (Zechariah 14:7).

The songs at Jennie's funeral services, led by the Chief Secretary, Colonel John W. Dent, at Thornbury Citadel and Fawkner Crematorium two days later reflected her strong faith in her Lord and Saviour.

How wonderful it is to walk with God
Along the road that holy men have trod;
How wonderful it is to hear him say:
Fear not, have faith, 'tis I who lead the way!

How wonderful 'twill be to live with God
When I have crossed death's deep and swelling flood;
How wonderful to see him face to face
When I have fought the fight and won the race![218]

When the shades of life are falling
And the hour has come to die,
Hear thy trusted leader calling:
I will guide thee with mine eye.[219]

--

There's a land that is fairer than day
And by faith we can see it afar;
For the Father waits over the way
To prepare us a dwelling place there.

In the sweet by-and-by
We shall meet on that beautiful shore.
In the sweet by-and-by
We shall meet on that beautiful shore.[220]

Both George and Jennie Lonnie were faithful and exemplary followers of their Lord, Jesus Christ, who would each have heard their Master's words, 'Well done, good and faithful servant'.

I believe they received, as the Apostle Peter wrote, 'an inheritance that can never perish, spoil or fade—kept in heaven for you, who through faith are shielded by God's power until the coming of the salvation that is already to be revealed in the last time. In this you greatly rejoice, though now for a little while you may have had to suffer grief in all kinds of trials. These have come so that your faith— of greater worth than gold, which perishes even though refined by fire—may be proved genuine and may result in praise, glory and honour when Jesus Christ is revealed' (1 Peter 1:4–7 NIV).

May all who read this account of their lives be encouraged to find this same lasting treasure and also follow Jesus faithfully, assured that, while the world may crown success, God crowns faithfulness.

Notes

Chapter 1 The carpenter from Yackandandah

1 Handwritten note by George Lonnie written at Brunswick Vic. in 1899, in possession of the author. His officer career card also indicates 10 November 1866.

2 Material drawn from *1856–1874 A History of Osbornes Flat SS No. 1463 1874–1974,* a booklet prepared for the celebration of the Centenary of the State School, original held by the Burke Memorial Museum, Family History Research Department, Beechworth, Vic.

3 Beechworth Corps records held at The Salvation Army Heritage Centre, Melbourne.

4 *The War Cry,* Melbourne, 15 October 1910, p. 6.

5 *The War Cry,* 30 August 1941, p. 6.

6 George Lonnie, *The War Cry,* 17 July 1926, p. 8.

7 Barbara Bolton: *Booth's Drum – The Salvation Army in Australia 1880–1980,* Sydney, Australia; Hodder and Stoughton, 1980, pp. 84–85.

8 ibid.

9 *The War Cry,* 15 October 1910, p. 6.

10 Holiness meetings were designed to provide worship, clear Bible teaching and encouragement to those who had made decisions for Christ toward the life of holiness and Christlikeness. These contrasted with Salvation meetings which were more evangelical in nature and designed to bring those who had not yet accepted Christ to a decision to follow him.

11 George Lonnie, *The War Cry,* 17 July, 1926, p. 8.

12 *The War Cry,* 15 October 1910, p. 6.

13 Photocopy in possession of the author.

14 *The War Cry,* 25 April 25 1908.

15 *The War Cry*, 15 October 1910, p. 6.

Chapter 2 Pioneering in the West

16 Apparently at a place called Fly Creek, according to Malcolm Uren, *The Glint of Gold* (Melbourne, Australia; Robertson & Mullens Limited, 1948), p. 159.
17 *The War Cry*, 7 April 1928.
18 Malcolm Uren, op. cit., p. 158.
19 'I look upon the whole world as my parish …' *John Wesley's Journal* 11 June 1739 noted in https://jamespedlar.wordpress.com/2011/05/21/four-john-wesley-quotes-everyone-should-know/ viewed 1 June 2017.
20 From the caption with an enlargement of this photograph on display at Coolgardie which the author photographed in 1992.
21 Brad Halse, 'The Salvation Army in Western Australia Its Early Years— "Ours is a very fast express train"' (Manuscript essay, 1990), p. 17.
22 V. Whittington, *Two Fevers, Gold and Typhoid*, Nedlands, UWA Press, 1988, p. 54, quoted in Halse, op. cit., p. 17.
23 Uren, op. cit., p. 158.
24 ibid., pp. 158–159.
25 Barbara Bolton, op. cit., p. 105.
26 Colonel Percival Dale, *Salvation Chariot*, Melbourne, The Salvation Army, 1952, p. 31.
27 The author has a copy of George Lonnie's marching orders, signed by the Territorial Commander in Melbourne on 29 October 1894 (probably because of his promotion to the rank of captain) and indicating that he should arrive in Wagin on 15 November.
28 E.M. Hasluck: 'The Drum Beats – Part History of the Salvation Army. Opening up the work in West Australia' (copy of manuscript provided to the author by The Salvation Army Archives, Western Australia), p. 8.
29 From a photograph of the gravestone supplied to the author by William (Bill) S. Booth, The Salvation Army Western Australia Archives.

Chapter 3 Elsewhere in Western and South Australia

30 The author also has a copy of Captain George Lonnie's marching orders, signed by the Divisional Officer, Major William Hunter, in

Perth on 25 June 1895 and indicating that he should arrive in Guildford on 4 July.

31 George Lonnie, *The War Cry,* 7 November, 1931, p. 4.

32 ibid.

33 Material from the *Northam Corps Centenary Book 1891–1991*, record from 1896, provided by The Salvation Army Western Australia Archives.

34 *The War Cry*, 7 November 1931, p. 9.

35 ibid.

36 ibid.

37 ibid.

38 ibid., p. 3.

39 From G.S.C.: '"Laying the tablets" – A Salvation Army building in old Kalgoorlie, 1897.' (A typewritten document provided by The Salvation Army Western Australia Archives), p. 1.

40 ibid., p. 2.

41 'Kalgoorlie Miner', 28 January 1897, p. 2. Copy in the possession of The Salvation Army Western Australia Archives, and typewritten copy provided to the author.

42 *The War Cry,* 15 October 1910, p. 6.

43 Sister Shirley Russell, Corps Secretary of Perth Fortress, found this information in the Corps History Book in October 2009 and was asked by the then Divisional Commander, Major Barry Casey, to pass this on to the author.

44 E.M. Hasluck, p. 3 suggests that that the tent was initially set up on the south-eastern corner of William and Newcastle Streets, Northbridge, Perth. He indicates that Temperance Hall in Museum Street was also used for time during that period of transition.

45 *The War Cry,* 15 October, 1910, p. 6.

46 *The War Cry,* 18 March 1899, p. 8.

Chapter 4 The children's worker from Ballarat

47 From the 'Index to Unassisted Inward Passenger Lists to Victoria 1852–1923', as at 28/12/2010.

48 According to the Marriage Certificate of Jennie Lonnie (nee Hammer).

49 ibid., Annie, although noted as Ann Brokenshire on the 'Index to Unassisted Inward Passenger Lists 1852–1923'.

50 According to George Lonnie's Officer Career Card, a copy in the author's possession.

51 Jennie Lonnie (Mrs Lieut-Colonel Lonnie): *The War Cry,* 19 February 1949, p. 9.

52 Letter from Brigadier Reuben Edwards to Ensign D. Sawkins, dated 29 March 1913, held at The Salvation Army Heritage Centre, Melbourne.

53 Colonel Percival Dale, op. cit., p. 39.

54 ibid., pp. 39–40.

55 Having encouraged the planting of both Soldier's Hill/Ballarat North Corps and Ballarat West Corps in 1890, Ballarat East was renamed Ballarat Central in 1917. Information from The Salvation Army Heritage Centre, Melbourne, 6 July 2017.

56 Jennie Lonnie, *The War Cry*, 19 February 1949.

57 ibid.

58 *The War Cry,* 10 December 1927.

59 ibid., 17 September 1927, p. 10.

60 Funeral tribute to Mrs Lieut-Colonel Jennie Lonnie, *The War Cry*, 29 May 1954, p. 3.

61 *The War Cry,* 1 September 1900, p. 24.

62 Jennie Lonnie, *The War Cry*, 19 February 1949.

63 ibid.

64 Baltimore, in *The War Cry,* 23 February 1901, p. 14.

65 *The War Cry,* 25 April 1908.

Chapter 5 New Zealand

66 Cyril R. Bradwell OF, in an article on 'New Zealand, Fiji and Tonga Territory' in Major John G. Merritt, *Historical Dictionary of the Salvation Army,* Lanham, Maryland; Toronto; Oxford; Scarecrow Press, 2006, p. 401.

67 *The War Cry*, New Zealand, 20 February 1904.

68 ibid.

69 Captain Mary Anderson, *The Young Soldier,* Australia, 11 March 1905, p. 12.

70 Information provided by Selwyn Bracegirdle, Research and Content Manager, The Salvation Army Heritage Centre & Archives, Booth College of Mission, 20 William Booth Grove, Upper Hutt 5018, New Zealand by email to the author on 10 October 2018.

71 Captain Mary Anderson, *The Young Soldier*, Australia, 11 March 1905, p. 12. To corroborate that Harry's funeral took place in Auckland, the Salvation Army New Zealand Archives confirmed that Staff-Captain Bishop was then appointed to the Prison Gate Home in Epsom, Auckland, and certainly not in Christchurch.

72 *The War Cry*, Melbourne, 25 February 1905, p. 8.

73 Frank Woodroffe, *The War Cry*, New Zealand, 4 March 1905.

74 Mrs Adjutant Lonnie, ibid., 9 September 1905; final poem anon.

75 H. Bramwell Cook: *Think on These Things – The Salvation Army Christchurch City Corps 1883–2008,* Christchurch, NZ; The Salvation Army Christchurch City Corps; 2008; p. 60.

76 *The War Cry*, New Zealand, 30 December 1905, p. 11.

77 Cook, op. cit., pp. 137–139.

78 ibid., p. 55.

79 *The War Cry*, New Zealand, 25 November 1905.

80 ibid.

81 ibid.

82 ibid., 24 November 1906

83 ibid., 5 May 1906.

84 ibid., 14 April 1906, p. 10.

85 ibid., 2 March 1907.

86 ibid., 31 August 1907.

87 ibid., 29 February 1908.

88 ibid., 25 January 1908.

89 ibid., 8 August 1908.

90 ibid., 9 May 1908.

91 New Zealand *Disposition of Forces* (information provided by The Salvation Army New Zealand, Fiji and Tonga Heritage Centre and Archives, 2017).

92 *The War Cry*, New Zealand, 16 May 1908.

93 ibid., 30 May 1908.

94 ibid., 19 September 1908.

95 ibid., 26 September 1908.

96 ibid., 7 November 1908.

97 ibid., 25 December 1909.

Chapter 6 Back in Australia – Sydney and Brisbane

98 *The War Cry*, Melbourne, 29 August 1910, p. 9.
99 ibid., Melbourne, 22 October 1910, p. 6.
100 ibid., 27 May 1911, p. 6.
101 ibid., 16 December 1911, p. 4.
102 ibid., 10 June 1911, p. 8.
103 ibid., 10 June 1911 p. 8 quoting from *The Sydney Morning Herald*.
104 ibid., 17 February 1912, pp. 9–11.
105 ibid., 16 March 1912, p. 12.
106 ibid., 21 December 1912, p. 14.
107 ibid., 14 October 1911, p. 3.
108 ibid., 4 May 1912, p. 3.
109 ibid., 7 December 1912, p. 11.
110 ibid., 28 December 1912, p. 14.
111 Cyril R. Bradwell, from *The Veteran*, New Zealand, Fiji and Tonga
    Territory, n.d. and quoted in *RO Zone*, January/February n.d., copy of
    page held by author.
112 *The War Cry*, 11 January 1913, p. 6.
113 ibid.

Chapter 7 Divisional leadership

114 *The War Cry*, Melbourne, 18 April 1916, p. 15.
115 ibid., 15 April 1916, p. 8.
116 ibid., 8 January 1916, p. 7.
117 ibid.
118 ibid., 13 February 1915, pp. 5–6.
119 ibid., 30 January 1915, p. 7.
120 ibid., 1 April 1916, p. 7.
121 ibid., 13 January 1917, p. 11.
122 ibid., 30 January 1915, p. 7.
123 ibid., 29 April 1916, p. 7.
124 ibid., 24 June 1916, p. 7.
125 ibid., 6 March 1915, p. 5.
126 ibid., 31 July 1915, p. 5, for example.
127 ibid., 8 January 1916, p. 7, and ibid., 24 June 1916, p. 7.
128 ibid., 7 April 1916, p. 7.

129 ibid.

130 ibid., 18 September 1915, p. 7.

131 ibid., 24 June 1916, p. 7.

132 ibid., 20 January 1917, p. 7.

133 ibid.

134 ibid., 27 January 1917, p. 7.

135 ibid.

136 ibid.

137 ibid., 19 May 1917, p. 7.

138 ibid., 8 January 1921, p. 3.

139 ibid., 19 February 1921, p. 3.

140 ibid., 23 April 23 1921, p. 6.

141 ibid.

142 ibid.

143 ibid.

144 ibid.

145 ibid., 7 May 1921, p. 7.

146 ibid., 2 May 1925.

147 ibid., 16 July 1925, p. 3.

148 ibid., 17 September 1921, p. 8.

149 ibid., 26 November 1921, p. 8.

150 ibid., 14 January 1922, p. 8.

151 ibid., 23 June 1923, p. 8.

152 ibid., 12 April 1924, p. 6.

153 ibid., 4 February 1922, p. 8, for instance.

154 *The Young Soldier*, 12 April 1924, p. 6

155 *The Victory*, 1 April 1924, p. 128.

156 *The War Cry*, Melbourne, 20 June 1925, p. 10.

157 ibid., 19 September 1925, p. 9.

158 ibid., 7 November 1925, p. 9.

159 ibid.

160 ibid.

Chapter 8 Territory-wide opportunities

161 ibid., 30 January 1926, p. 1.

162 *The Young Soldier,* 10 April 1926, p. 2.

163 *The War Cry,* Melbourne, 10 April, 1926, p. 9.

164 ibid., 17 July 1926, p. 8.

165 ibid.

166 ibid.

167 ibid.

168 ibid.

169 ibid.

170 ibid., 1 January 1927, p. 6.

171 ibid., 5 March 1927, p. 10.

172 Identification of Major Dean as Major Percy Dean confirmed by The Salvation Army Heritage Centre in Melbourne, October 2017 from ibid., 10 August 1923, p. 6; and 3 November 1923.

173 ibid., 19 February 1927, p. 10; 26 February 1927, p. 10; 5 March 1927, p.7.

174 ibid., 27 August 1927, p. 10.

175 ibid., 3 September 1927, p. 8.

176 ibid., 17 September 1927, p. 10.

177 ibid.

178 ibid., 27 August 1927, p. 8.

179 ibid.

180 ibid.

181 ibid.

182 ibid.

183 ibid., 29 October 1927, p. 8.

184 ibid., 31 March 1928, p. 9.

185 ibid.

186 ibid., 21 January 1928, p. 8.

187 ibid., 10 December 1927, p. 6.

188 ibid.

189 Jennie Lonnie, ibid., 11 February 1928, p. 8.

190 *The War Cry*, Melbourne, 14 July 1928, p. 10.

191 ibid., 19 May 1928, p. 10.

192 Jennie Lonnie, *The War Cry*, Melbourne, 10 March 1928, p. 3.

193 ibid.

194 Jennie Lonnie, *The War Cry*, Melbourne, 13 October 1928, p. 9.

195 ibid.

196 ibid.

197 ibid., 1 June 1929, p. 10.

198 *The War Cry*, Melbourne, 15 June 1929, p. 9.

199 ibid., 8 June 1929, p.10.

200 ibid., 15 June 1929, p. 10; 22 June 1929, p. 10; 13 July 1929, p. 10; 5 October 1929, p. 10; 19 October 1929, p. 10.

201 From a copy of his Career Card, in possession of the author.

202 Various reports in *The War Cry* in 1930.

203 *The War Cry*, Melbourne, 29 November 1930, p. 8.

204 ibid., 23 August 1930, p. 12.

205 ibid., 5 April 1930, p. 6.

206 ibid., 13 September 1930, p. 10.

207 ibid., 18 July 1931, p. 10.

208 ibid.

Chapter 9 Retirement

209 ibid., 7 November 1931, p. 3.

210 ibid., p. 4.

211 ibid., p. 3.

212 *Ballarat Courier*, 'Salvation Army Worker Farewelled', c. 1932. Photocopy in possession of the author.

213 *The Argus*, Melbourne, Vic. Monday, 31 December 1934, p. 12, (http:nla.gov.au/nla.news-article11004260).

214 ibid.

215 *The War Cry*, Melbourne, 21 November 1936, p. 16.

216 ibid., 1943, p. 4.

217 Copy in possession of the author.

218 Theodore Hopkins Kitching (1866–1930), *The Song Book of The Salvation Army* (2015), Song 838.

219 Nathaniel Niles (1835–1917), ibid., Song 669.

220 Sanford Fillmore Bennett (1836–1898), ibid., Song 552.

221 Definitions adapted from *The Salvation Army Year Book 2016*, London, UK; Salvation Books, The Salvation Army International Headquarters, 2015, pp. 18–20; also 12, 34–36 with permission of The General of The Salvation Army.

Glossary of some Salvation Army Terms and Abbreviations used in this book[221]

Articles of War: Earlier name for the Soldier's Covenant (see below).

Cadet: A Salvationist who is in training for officership.

Candidate: A soldier who has been accepted for officer training.

Chief Secretary (CS): The officer second-in-command of the Army in a territory.

Commission: A document presented publicly, authorising an officer or local officer to fulfil a specified ministry.

Congress: Central gathering which is often held annually and attended by most officers and many soldiers of the territory, command, region or division.

Corps: A Salvation Army unit established for the preaching of the gospel, worship, teaching and fellowship and to provide Christian-motivated service in the community. Corps is The Salvation Army term for a church or congregation.

Dedication Service: A public presentation of infants to the Lord. This differs from christening or infant baptism in that the main emphasis is upon specific vows made by the parents concerning the child's upbringing.

Division: A number of corps grouped together under the direction of a divisional commander operating within a territory.

Divisional Commander (DC): The officer in charge of the Army in a division.

Divisional Secretary (DS): The officer second in charge of the Army in a division.

Envoy: A Salvationist whose duty it is to visit corps, societies and outposts for the purpose of conducting meetings. An envoy may be appointed in charge of any such unit.

General: The officer elected to the supreme command of the Army throughout the world. All appointments are made and all regulations issued under the General's authority.

Home League (HL): Part of the Women's Ministries of The Salvation Army in which Christian influence is exerted and practical help given for the benefit of the individual, the family and the nation.

International Headquarters (IHQ): The office in London, UK, at which the official business of the Army around the world is transacted.

Mercy Seat: A bench provided as a place where people can kneel to pray, seeking salvation or sanctification, or making a special consecration to God's will and service. The mercy seat is usually situated between the platform and main area of Army halls and is the focal point to remind all of God's reconciling and redeeming presence.

Officer: A Salvationist who has been trained, commissioned and ordained to service and leadership in response to God's call. An officer is a recognised minister of religion.

Order of the Founder (OF): The highest Salvation Army honour for distinguished service.

Outpost: A locality in which Army work is carried out and where it is hoped a society or corps will develop.

Pastoral Care Council (PCC; previously known as the Census Board): Established in each corps for the care of soldiers, etc., and maintenance of membership rolls.

Promotion to Glory (pG): The Army's description of the death of Salvationists.

Ranks of Officers: Lieutenant, captain, major, lieut-colonel, colonel, commissioner, General. *Previous ranks* have included: ensign, adjutant, staff-captain, field-major, senior-captain, senior-major, brigadier and lieut-commissioner.

Red Shield: A symbol saying 'The Salvation Army' in the local language, identifying personnel, buildings, equipment, mobile units and emergency services.

Salvation: The work of grace which God accomplishes in a repentant person whose trust is in Christ as Saviour, forgiving sin, giving new direction to life and strength to live as God desires.

Self Denial Appeal (SD or SDA): An annual effort by Salvationists and friends to raise funds for the Army's worldwide operations.

Sergeant: A local officer appointed for specific duty, usually in a corps.

Society: A company of soldiers who work together regularly in a district, without an officer.

Soldier: A converted person of at least 14 years of age who has, with the approval of the Senior Pastoral Care Council, been enrolled (and publicly sworn-in) as a member of The Salvation Army after signing the Soldier's Covenant.

Soldier's Covenant: The statement of beliefs and promises which every intending soldier is required to sign before enrolment. Previously called the 'Articles of War'.

Territorial Commander (TC): The officer in command of the Army in a territory.

Territory: A country, part of a country or several countries combined, in which Salvation Army work is organised under a territorial commander.

Territorial Headquarters (THQ): The office at which the official business of the territory is transacted.

Young People's Sergeant-Major (YPSM): A local officer responsible for young people's work in a corps, under the commanding officer.

Bibliography

Ballarat Courier, 1932.

Beechworth Corps records held at The Salvation Army Archives and Museum, Melbourne.

Bolton, Barbara, *Booth's Drum: The Salvation Army in Australia 1880– 1980,* Sydney, Australia; Hodder and Stoughton, 1980.

1856–1874 A History of Osbornes Flat SS No. 1463 1874–1974, a booklet prepared for the celebration of the Centenary of the State School, original held by the Burke Memorial Museum, Family History Research Department, Beechworth, Vic.

Bradwell, Cyril R., from *The Veteran*, New Zealand, Fiji and Tonga Territory, n.d. and quoted in *RO Zone*, January/February n.d. copy of page held by author.

Cook, H. Bramwell, *Think on These Things: The Salvation Army Christchurch City Corps 1883–2008,* Christchurch, NZ; The Salvation Army Christchurch City Corps, 2008.

Dale, Colonel Percival, *Salvation Chariot*, Melbourne, The Salvation Army, 1952.

G.S.C., '"Laying the tablets" – A Salvation Army building in old Kalgoorlie, 1897.' (A typewritten document provided by The Salvation Army, Western Australia Archives).

Halse, Brad, 'The Salvation Army in Western Australia Its Early Years—"Ours is a very fast express train"' (Manuscript essay, 1990).

Hasluck, E.M., 'The Drum Beats – Part History of the Salvation Army. Opening up the work in West Australia' (copy of manuscript provided to the author by The Salvation Army Archives, Western Australia).

'Index to Unassisted Inward Passenger Lists to Victoria 1852–1923', as at 28/12/2010.

'Kalgoorlie Miner', 28 January 1897, p. 2. Copy in the possession of The Salvation Army Western Australia Archives, and typewritten copy provided to the author.

Merritt, Major John G., *Historical Dictionary of the Salvation Army*, Lanham, Maryland; Toronto; Oxford; Scarecrow Press, 2006.

New Zealand Salvation Army *Disposition of Forces* (information provided by The Salvation Army New Zealand, Fiji and Tonga Heritage Centre and Archives, 2017).

Northam Corps Centenary Book 1891–1991, record from 1896, provided by The Salvation Army Western Australia Archives.

The Argus, Melbourne, Vic., Monday, 31 December 1934, p. 12, http:nla.gov.au/nla.news-article11004260.

The Songbook of The Salvation Army, The General of The Salvation Army, London, United Kingdom, 2015.

The Victory, The Salvation Army, Australia, 1924.

The War Cry, The Salvation Army, Australia, 1894, 1896, 1899, 1900, 1901, 1904, 1905, 1906, 1907, 1908, 1909, 1910, 1911, 1912, 1913, 1915, 1916, 1917, 1921, 1922, 1923, 1924, 1925, 1926, 1927, 1928, 1929, 1930, 1931, 1936, 1941, 1949, 1954.

The War Cry, The Salvation Army, New Zealand, 1904, 1905, 1906, 1907, 1908, 1909.

The Young Soldier, The Salvation Army, Australia, 1905, 1924.

Uren, Malcolm, *The Glint of Gold,* Melbourne, Australia, Robertson & Mullens Limited, 1948.

Wesley, John, *John Wesley's Journal,* 11 June 1739 noted in https://jamespedlar.wordpress.com/2011/05/21/four-john-wesley-quotes-everyone-should-know/ viewed 1 June 2017.

Whittington, V., *Two Fevers, Gold and Typhoid,* Nedlands, UWA Press, 1988.

About The Author

Lieut-Colonel Ian Southwell is the son of Australian Salvation Army officers and a grandson of George and Jennie Lonnie. Ian was a university-trained science and mathematics teacher before marrying his wife Sonja in 1967 and training together to become officers in the late 1960s. Their joint service has taken them around the world as outlined in their book, *Safely Led to Serve: A Joint Biography* (Balboa Press, 2017). Now retired from active service, Ian and Sonja are involved in pastoral, interchurch, literary and other ministries on behalf of The Salvation Army in Melbourne, Australia. Ian and Sonja have three daughters, all involved in helping ministries, one of whom is also a Salvation Army officer.

Lasting Treasure
www.facebook.com/lastingtreasurebook

Printed in the United States
By Bookmasters